ANCESTORS

ANCESTORS

The Loving Family in Old Europe

STEVEN OZMENT

HARVARD UNIVERSITY PRESS
CAMBRIDGE, MASSACHUSETTS
LONDON, ENGLAND
2001

Library of Congress Cataloging-in-Publication Data

Ozment, Steven E.
Ancestors : the loving family in old Europe / Steven Ozment.
p. cm.
Includes bibliographical references and index.
ISBN 0-674-00483-3 (cloth : alk. paper)—ISBN 0-674-00484-1 (paper : alk. paper)
1. Family—Europe—History. 2. Family—Europe—Historiography. I. Title.

HQ611 .O968 2001
306.85′094—dc21   00-063447

To Carolyn for her constancy
and Kerry for the cake

CONTENTS

Illustrations follow page 76.

ANCESTORS

INTRODUCTION

As every good historian will tell you, the past is a distant place. Today, as perhaps never before, the otherness of the past is stressed in historical study, and not only because it presents us with a strange and different world. Many also believe that world still to be a dangerous and threatening one for people living today. Those who venture too close to it risk being pulled back into a past of fixed essences and hierarchies over which all-knowing political and religious elites rule—a combination deadly to modern liberty and equality. From this perspective, the past becomes a world we are fortunate to have lost and properly continue to flee.[1]

Every good historian will also tell you that the past is inescapable, forgotten by a present generation at the latter's peril. If today is the first day of the rest of one's life, it is even more the last day to date of the history of human civilization. The centuries that lie behind us are a deep, clinical record of human behavior, while the lessons still to be learned about ourselves from centuries to come exist only in our imaginations. From this perspective, the greater temptation for every generation is not slippage back into the past, but belief that past, present, and future constitute absolutely different periods of time and fundamentally distinct types of humanity. *Ancestors* presupposes that human life is continuous, integrated from century to century and from generation to generation, and that knowledge of a land or a people's historical evolution, no matter how near or far back it goes, always helps that land or people make sense of the present-day world.

The centuries between 1400 and 1800 have long been the battleground for defining the emergence of the "modern" European family in terms of its structure, organization, and private life. These are centuries in which historians discern a new family type emerging and displacing the family as it had existed since antiquity. For most, it is over the eighteenth and nineteenth centuries that the new family becomes pervasive, and during the twentieth it is said to have been set irreversibly in place. Its defining conditions and features are fourfold: the separation of home and workplace (parents begin to work in factories or offices, allowing the home to become a special place); the departure of servants and workers from the household and a new prominence of the nuclear family, or parent-child unit; that family's withdrawal from public life ("cocooning"); and a growing recognition of spousal equality and sharing of authority within a family-centered rather than a work-centered environment.[2] Only as these four conditions were met, it is argued, could the history of the family become a progressive one, and the family as we know it today a reality.

Juxtaposed to this triumphant modern family is a premodern, or preindustrial, counterpart most people today will thank their lucky stars they did not grow up in. Exceedingly vulnerable to the tyranny of man and nature, the family of old adopted a rigid internal organization for its own protection—one that is said to have been hostile to democracy, the emancipation of women, and the gratification of children. Forced to concentrate its energies on feeding and protecting itself, this challenged family logically evolved into an impersonal household, ruled over by an imperious patriarch to whom all members were subordinate and subject, and in which relatives and kin were as much family as the parent-child unit, and often more so. The psychic and moral costs of this domestic arrangement are said to have been exceedingly high for subsequent history: an inability of household members to establish bonds of deep affection or relationships of true equality, regardless of degree of kinship or familiarity among the inmates.

This portrayal of the premodern family is largely the creation of an influential group of scholars writing in the 1960s and 1970s. Their counterparts in the 1980s and 1990s have since drawn very different conclusions about the premodern family. *Ancestors* attempts to highlight the differences between the two sides and make clear the possibilities this confrontation has opened, both for future scholarly research and for a modern society that finds itself in the throes of a family crisis.

STRUCTURE AND SENTIMENT

Following the lead of the social sciences, the modern study of the family has focused on group organization and behavior within a presumably integrated social and cultural world. This is especially true of the "household economics" approach to family history, which attempts to explain human behavior and relationships through larger structures and constraints that often go unrecognized by the multitudes they silently influence.[1] The challenge here is to typify or model a larger society and culture before addressing finite subjects within it—this in the reasonable belief that what surrounds a subject may also best explain it. As demographers have demonstrated, a great deal can be written about the size and composition of households without walking through the door of a single house or delving into the private life of any one family. And not a few generalizations about the inner life of families have been extrapolated from sparse or controversial quantitative data.[2]

The study of the family through its structures and numbers has increased the excitement of family history and given it a quasi-scientific appearance. Preoccupation with the family's surface similarities and patterns, however, has made it more difficult for historians to see the faces and hear the voices of the subjects themselves, who easily become lost in the semantic greenery of an ever enlarging theoretical forest.[3]

Further complicating the family historian's task is a powerful argument that a family is more an ongoing moral experiment than any fixed, predictable institution,[4] and as such a poor mirror of society at large. Historians wishing to avoid societal blurring of family life and unfounded generalization about it find it prudent to anchor their studies in family archives, whose sources provide deeper access to the subjects themselves and the actual worlds they inhabit. Even though the data collected in these archives are limited to a particular family, they are neither irrelevant to the study of an age nor without application to a larger society. Houses have windows and doors, and the burgher households of the past were even busier crossroads of contemporary society than are their present-day counterparts.

Still, there probably can never be enough studies of individual families to justify confident generalizations about "the family" across society and over time in any one age. As a rule of thumb, the more detailed the study of a particular family, the more difficult it becomes to generalize from it, while the less penetrating the study of actual families across a society, the more fecund an overarching theory. That may explain in part why "deep interpretation," which is theory driven, triumphed so completely over "deep sourcing," which relies on many layers of reasonable fact, in the work of the historians we will meet in the first part of this book.

That being said, it is neither the bias of historians nor the human predilection to treat people in distant ages or cultures as basically the same that poses the greatest obstacle to making sound historical generalizations about the family. The main problem lies in the nature of families themselves. A family is not a standard product of some universal social mix, but an organization of discrete individuals interacting with one another in a sui generis familial world created by and large by that interaction. Yet, although families have been freely opening and closing doors to the larger outside world since the beginning of human civilization, many today view them as thoroughly integrated social units and hence reliable reflections of a larger surrounding world. Herein lies the origin of the treatment of the family as a mirror of the body politic, a microcosm of mass culture, even a true image and docile servant of the state. Yet the evidence remains overwhelming that local, territorial, and state governments from antiquity to the present have remained very limited in their ability to mold domestic behavior and control society at its grass roots, where unruliness has proven to be the rule. When people in medieval and early modern Europe thought about the continuity of society, they thought less about a centralized "state," which was then still evolving, than they did about the succession and success of individual members within their own household and among their own kin.[5]

At the same time, individual families have understandably been taken to represent some distant ages simply because of the limited sources available for the study of those ages. Existing records for the family in periods of antiquity and the Middle Ages rarely allow historians to delve much deeper than a royal or a noble family's formal political alliances and public ceremonies. Under such circumstances, family history necessarily becomes a study of caste, clan, and lineage in family formation around the patriline, or an ambitious effort to discern the genuine domestic and social residues in clerically composed saints' lives.[6] Here, what cannot be deeply known must unfortunately remain the whole story.

Not until the fifteenth century did the requisite education and tools needed to write and preserve detailed family histories become widely available to the urban lay public, resulting in the creation of family archives of such quantity and quality that truly penetrating studies of the inner life of the premodern family became possible.[7] For the first time on a large scale, and at heretofore unreachable levels, the inner circle of the family and the private lives of individuals within a household became visible beneath their external structure and organization.

The House that Philippe Ariès Built

The person who has done the most to shape our present-day view of the family, past and present, is French scholar Philippe Ariès (1914–1984). In a famous study published in 1960,[8] Ariès presented a paradoxical argument, both sides of which portrayed the children of the past as victims of parents and society. On the one hand, children were said to have been treated as "little adults," while on the other, the adult world's progressive discovery of childhood as a special stage of life begat an unholy desire in parents and society to mold their children into perfect adults, thereby making those children's lives actually worse than before.

Ariès closely associated the rise of the modern family with the demise of service and apprenticeship as society's way of educating its young. The "essential event" was the progressive shift of vocational training from faraway homes and shops to nearby schools over the course of the seventeenth century. That, Ariès believed, gave parents longer contact and deeper involvement with their children, who were henceforth no longer to be "abandoned [to others] at the tender age of seven."

> The sentimental climate was [now] entirely different and closer to our [own], as if the modern family originated at the same time as the school, [which] satisfied both the desire for a theoretical education to replace the old practical forms of apprenticeship, and the desire of parents to keep their children near home for as long as possible. This phenomenon . . . bears witness to a major transformation of the family: it fell back upon the child, and its life became identified with the increasingly sentimental relationship between parents and children.[9]

Although the breakthrough came in the seventeenth century, Ariès recognized signs of a dawning "new sensibility" as early as the thirteenth,[10] evidence of which he found in realistic child portraiture, children's apparel, games, and pastimes, parental efforts to segregate children from adult society, and, by the sixteenth century, the reproval of parents for coddling their children.[11] Such signs, however, were only straws in a fickle wind; the family's emotional detachment from its children could not be overcome until three controlling circumstances changed: high child mortality,[12] the integration of home and workplace, and the near total absence of privacy within households. Taken together, these conditions encouraged parents to look on their children as latent adults and to treat them as such "as soon as a child could live without the constant solicitude of his mother, his nanny, or cradle-rocker."[13]

Ariès emphatically denied that parents in the past consciously "neglected, forsook, or despised" their children. It was not love that went missing in the premodern household, but parental and societal "awareness of the particular nature of childhood" and with it care for and involvement in a child's life.[14] Parents in the past simply did not recognize their children as such; the premodern family was only a "moral and social unit," not yet a sentimental one.[15]

The retention of the child in the home for a longer period of time proved also to have a dark side: the family now began to withdraw from society and turn inward upon itself. Before this point was reached in the seventeenth century, Ariès believed the family had been a remarkably gregarious and charitable institution, readily deferring to and embracing the world around it.[16] That very communal allegiance had been the major impediment to the development of a vital private life. Thus, in Ariès's scheme, nothing signaled the arrival of the modern family more than the triumph of privacy over sociability.[17] However, what children now gained in attention and care, they progressively lost in freedom and tranquility. The new family and the new schools saved them from a premature adulthood only to deprive them of the leisure and informality they had enjoyed as little adults. "The birch and the prison cell" replaced parental indifference, and the old society's tolerance and diversity diminished under heightened preoccupation with discipline and conformity.[18] Reared in homes and schools more intent than ever on "cultivating" them, children would now grow up to be less joyous adults.

Despite such argument, Ariès could still describe his strongest empirical evidence (the placement of children at tender ages in apprenticeship, school, and service) as an act of self-sacrificial love in the minds of the parents themselves. Nor were children as a rule put out to new masters casually and without protective covenants. As contemporary letters might also have reminded Ariès, an absent child's bonds with parents and siblings could also deepen with the greater maturity such separations occasioned.[19] If Ariès could find modern sentimentality dawning in sixteenth-century criticism of primogeniture, he should logically also have acknowledged its shining as early as the twelfth century in medieval law codes mandating equitable distribution of family wealth to all offspring.[20] There is also an argument to be made that a family's sociability and sentimentality can be two sides of the same emotion, a simultaneous pursuit of communal obligations and private interests without any sense of contradiction or the mutually incapacitating consequences Ariès alleged.

Over the almost forty years since the publication of *Centuries of Childhood,* many scholars and pundits, and through them a sizable segment of the general public, have embraced Ariès's basic argument with slight modification. Five of the most influential scholars of the family are among them: Viennese historians Michael Mitterauer and Reinhard Sieder, American sociologist Edward Shorter, French historian Jean-Louis Flandrin, and English historian Lawrence Stone, each of whom wrote a major work of family history during the 1970s.

Michael Mitterauer and Reinhard Sieder

Hailed as the authoritative family history for German-speaking lands, Mitterauer and Sieder's study of the European family[21] parted ways with Ariès on only two points: the date of the arrival of the modern sentimental family (eighteenth and nineteenth centuries rather than the seventeenth and eighteenth) and the clear moral superiority of that family over its predecessor (on which Ariès was ambivalent). Mitterauer and Sieder's modern German family, like Ariès's, was child-centered, jealous of its privacy, and mindful of each member's individuality and rights. And the forces giving rise to it were also Ariès's: a strengthening relationship between parents and children, the release of servants and boarders from the household, the rapid growth in the number of nuclear families, and above all the separation of home and workplace.[22]

So obsessed with household maintenance and security and bereft of "tenderness and loving intimacy" did the authors imagine the preindustrial family to be that they concluded that only the leisured, higher classes could have lived under conditions that permitted even sex to be enjoyed.[23] The emotionally challenged family of the past would not find relief until urbanization and industrialization put the state in a position to assume more of what had been the family's all-consuming protective and productive functions, which allowed large segments of society at last to relax, turn inward, and nurture an emotional life that had never received the attention it required.[24] Thanks to the separation of home and workplace, a new, egalitarian family structure could now develop, one in which women might enjoy equality, youth "recuperate their psychic energies," and all family members live and rule together as "partners." Here Mitterauer and Sieder saw the beginning of an "irreversible secular process" leading directly to the emancipation of women, children, and servants in the modern world.[25]

Edward Shorter

Caricature of the premodern family and idealization of its modern counterpart reached new heights in Edward Shorter's *The Making of the Modern Family* (1975). If, in the past, youth submitted too quickly to parents, wives to husbands, and families to the state, an immediate end to "superordinate and subordinate relations," whether in spousal or parent-child relationships, became the rallying cry of the modern family in this popular counterculture book.[26] Never again would wives docilely be treated "primarily as baby-machines . . . mechanically and without affection" by their husbands, nor parents succumb to the "often hideously hurtful infant hygiene and child-rearing practices" that were the norm in the premodern family.[27]

For Shorter, who grew up in the hot, rebellious 1960s, nothing better illustrated the successful tyranny of the premodern family than the "resolutely unerotic" lives it made its young lead. Well into the eighteenth century, he maintained, sex in the traditional family was only "instrumental," more a duty than a pleasure for most people.[28]

Jean-Louis Flandrin

In pursuit of changing concepts of childhood, Ariès set a high standard for creative documentation by reaching beyond student life to include children's portraiture, dress, games, and pastimes among his sources. Who, however, would have thought that the teaching manuals of celibate theologians, in which the questions to be asked of the laity at confession were formulated, might allow scholars to date precisely the emergence of the modern family?

Although counterintuitive on its face, given the Church's "monarchical" model of family life, French historian Jean-Louis Flandrin argued that changes he found in such manuals between 1500 and 1800 both indicated and instigated two definitive transformations of family life: the replacement of "mastery" by "companionship" in spousal relations and the eclipsing of parental rights by parental duties in parent-child relations.[29] Whereas before 1688 priests censured husbands who failed to police their wives' morals, by the eighteenth century they were telling wives to police their own morals and inquiring if they had done all that they might to preserve those of their husbands. The subject of spousal corporal punishment—the permitted "moderate" beating of wayward or disobedient wives after all else failed—now vanished completely from church manuals. Even cooperation between husband and wife in contraceptive strategy (mostly coitus interruptus) gained tacit approval from clergy and laity, who justified it as a deeper interpretation of the Christian ethic of love.

Flandrin drew a contrarian thesis from the confessional manuals he surveyed over three centuries: the cumulative weight of medieval Christian moral teaching, not the secular forces released by the Enlightenment and the French Revolution, laid the essential foundations for the rise of the modern sentimental, egalitarian family. In that judgment he included Protestants as well as Catholics: English Puritans were found to be a century ahead of Catholics in sanctioning romantic love between spouses and in stressing parental obligations toward children.[30]

Flandrin's sources also documented a "fundamental inversion" of the principles of familial morality in late-seventeenth-century parent-child relationships. For the first time on a large scale, contended Flandrin, parents viewed their children primarily as individuals requiring love and care rather than as creatures over whom they held inalienable rights.[31]

Some may think it incredible that the Church could, over centuries, inadvertently "structure the mentality of the laity" so as to undermine a model of family life it had championed for a millennium and a half, and to do so to the point of encouraging contraceptive practices it had always condemned. A more persuasive, if less kind, explanation of the Church's role in the rise of the modern family may be that the Church belatedly and even grudgingly accommodated new sentiments and practices that were in truth as old as human nature and had been developing at a healthy pace on their own well before priests began to intervene and presume to manage them.

Lawrence Stone

While agreeing that the seventeenth century was particularly decisive, Ariès's successors shifted the chronological hunting grounds for the modern family forward by two hundred years and reduced them by a century (from 1300–1700 to 1500–1800). At the same time, those successors also traced a revolution in family life that was far larger and less ambiguous than Ariès envisioned. Of subsequent studies alleging such a revolution by the seventeenth century, none carried Ariès's theses to and beyond their logical conclusion more dazzlingly than did Lawrence Stone in his evolutionary scheme of English family development put forth in *The Family, Sex, and Marriage in England, 1500–1800* (1977). Stone posited three precise, but overlapping chronological periods, each of which presented a predominant, yet still evolving discrete family type.

The first he called the "open lineage family" (1450–1630), or the family as it might be reconstructed from late-fifteenth and sixteenth-century sources. Unconcerned about privacy and individuality, this family was devoted far more to relatives and kin than to emotional bonding within the "loose association of transients" that then made up the household.[32] In an age when a quarter to a third of children died before their fifteenth birthday, the family was pervaded by "low gradient affect" and a "general psychological atmosphere of distance, manipulation, and deference." Beyond the effects of high child mortality, that conclusion was also documented by allegedly misguided child-rearing practices: the swaddling of infants; their placement with wet nurses for the first fourteen to eighteen months of life; methodical parental efforts to break a child's will in early childhood; and the placement of children between the ages of seven and ten in service and apprenticeship outside the home. In these early years, such "standard" child-rearing practices are said to have created "many adults whose primary responses to others were at best a calculating indifference."[33]

In Stone's scheme, the open lineage family was succeeded by a "restricted patriarchal nuclear family" (1550–1700). This type of family exhibited a higher degree of intimacy and affection within the parent-child relationship, which now began to hold priority over kin and the local community. Spanning and reflecting the religious and political upheavals of the age (the English Reformation and Revolution), this new family type was more inward-looking and controlling than its predecessor.[34] One result was improvement in spousal relations; the reformers, particularly the Puritans, exalted marriage for its emotional bonding and lifelong companionship.[35] However, this gain in family life was offset by the reformers' repressive child-rearing practices, which were based on belief in original sin and absolute parental control, and encouraged parents to flog and frighten their children into good behavior.[36]

"Steep gradient affect," the defining mark of the modern sentimental family, first appeared with the emergence of a "closed domesticated nuclear family" (1640–1800).[37] Marriage was now destined to be a progressively egalitarian institution, as spouses chose one another with greater care and their mutual rights and responsibilities were recognized by both genders. Husbands now addressed their wives by their first names and described them as their "best friends," and endearing terms became a fixture of family life.[38] In place of the harsh Christian view of infants as natural-born sinners came John Locke's view of them as starting life with a completely clean slate. Loose clothing replaced swaddling, maternal breast-feeding wet-nursing, encouragement the rod, and unabashed indulgence methodical efforts to break a child's will.[39]

By such happy argument and even happier prose, Stone turned Ariès's somber, tentative thesis into an unambiguous account, neatly piling the negative features of English family life onto the earlier centuries (the open lineage family), while shoving the positive ones into the later (the closed domesticated nuclear family). Although he attempted, perhaps ungraciously, to distinguish his own work from Ariès's by criticizing the latter's slippery historical methods,[40] Stone's own portrayal of English family life has been hailed as documenting the Frenchman's basic themes for England better than Ariès had been able to do for France.[41] In Stone, the Arièsian myth of the evolutionary development of the sentimental family over centuries had gained a precision and a glow it could never have had for its author, who believed that when the family fell in love with itself in the late seventeenth century, it became a lesser and a less interesting social institution.[42]

❦ 2 ❧

A GENDERED VIEW
OF FAMILY LIFE

With the exception of Ariès, each of the historians mentioned in the preceding chapter believed that the family changed unambiguously for the better between 1500 and 1800. All saw the first steps from "patriarchy to partnership" occurring at this time and believed that this development promised to make the relationship between men and women, husbands and wives, and parents and children both kinder and more equal. Over the same decades in which that argument was being made, a new breed of historian, devoted to reconstructing the contemporary woman's point of view, was also taking her first look at these same centuries strictly from the perspective of gender.[1] That scrutiny has since produced a rival chronology of debit and gain, which, while also not friendly to the premodern family, provocatively challenges some conclusions of the magisterial family historians of the 1960s and 1970s.

Whatever the centuries between 1500 and 1800 may have meant for the family, when weighed on the scales of gender they appear to have been a low point in the history of European women. By contrast, the preceding three centuries (1200–1500), traditionally treated by historians as calamitous for all, are now said to have been perhaps the best for women before the twentieth.[2]

In the 1970s, Natalie Zemon Davis articulated what has remained the acid test of significant historical progress for women: the "elimination of the[ir] subject status" measured by equivalent legal standing and career opportunities with men.[3] Particularly in the workplace, the earlier centuries offered women greater access to careers in industry and commerce outside the home—a development that had, however, very little to do with any radical enlightenment, new morality, or contemporary women's movement. It was rather contemporary society's response to demographic and economic changes beyond the control of men and women alike.

Working Women

During the thirteenth and fourteenth centuries, particularly in the half century after the Black Death (1350–1400), production in urban shops and industries expanded well beyond the available male work force, and this provided unprecedented opportunities for women to learn and practice a trade. Women's presence in the workaday world had already become commonplace and unquestioned during the previous 150 years of urban growth and boom. At the beginning of the fourteenth century, only three Parisian guilds explicitly excluded women. At the end of the fifteenth century, sixty-five of Frankfurt am Main's professions, mostly in the food, handwork (sewing, lace-making), and health industries, employed only women— eighty-one belonged exclusively to men; seventeen others saw women in the majority; and in thirty-eight, men and women worked together in roughly equal numbers.[4] In late medieval Cologne, women's guilds of yarn makers, gold and silk embroiderers, and silk makers were among the city's most labor-intensive and highly paid.[5]

In these centuries all women, including those in religious orders, also performed expected domestic chores, from gardening and cooking to sewing and cleaning. However, no division of labor along strict gender lines confined women to that work alone, while awarding income-producing careers outside the home exclusively to men.[6] After marriage, artisan and mercantile couples routinely worked together in home-based businesses, the wife often under her own direction, marketing co-produced wares to local shops and even traveling and selling

24

them at distant fairs. No one took offense when a woman operated the official weigh station in a particular town's markethouse.[7] Not only were large numbers of single and married women professionally employed in the late Middle Ages, women in religious and quasi-religious vocations undertook such work as well. In the cities of northern Germany, Holland, and Belgium, single women by the thousands lived communally as beguines in convents as small as four and larger than a hundred. Mid-thirteenth-century Cologne had 2,000 women in 163 convents, most supporting themselves as laundresses, brewers, bakers, weavers, and spinners.[8] Dutch and Belgian convents acquired such wealth by decorative sewing and lace work that some lent money advantageously to city governments and became unwelcome competitors with local guilds.[9]

The equality late medieval women enjoyed at home and in the workplace is attested by their legal rights. Although a married woman remained under her husband's authority *(Munt)* at home, in practice, she played the matriarch to his patriarch, "wearing the pants" in the household, as both, together and independently, planned and directed their shared household and business obligations.[10] Thanks to numerous shops able to supply inexpensive food and clothing to working spouses, and the many helping hands of older children, maids, and servants, urban wives at the end of the Middle Ages were hardly drudges.[11]

Through her husband, an urban wife enjoyed full, if "passive," citizenship *(Bürgerrecht)*, giving her the same protections and privileges he enjoyed, with the notable exception of direct participation in politics and government, which Western women did not enjoy until the twentieth century. Such citizenship was denied the masses of nonpropertied males, while propertied widows could buy it. Both housefather and housemother could command servants and authorize them to buy goods and contract services for the household. A wife also had oversight of all members of the household, and the property she brought to the marriage could not be disposed of without her consent.[12]

A husband with just cause, however, could in law physically discipline a wife, much as he might do a servant or a child. Until the fifteenth century, men in many lands held the power of life and death over wives caught in adultery, whereas women had no such reciprocal right. Contemporary illustrations depict husbands running an unfaithful wife and her male lover through with a single thrust of a sword after having caught the two in the missionary position.[13]

Still, in criminal matters, a victimized woman had equal access to the courts and justice, as crimes against women threatened social order as much as crimes against men. Just how principled a late medieval court might be in cases of rape and violence against women is illustrated by the fourteenth-century code of Advocate Ruprecht of Friesling (1328), which contained a provision for an ordeal to settle cases that failed the strict test of evidence and jury trial. The accused man was made to stand in a pit the width of a wagon wheel up to his navel and to fight with a club, while the plaintiff circled him with a sling-like mace made by placing a large stone in her head scarf. Few women appear to have taken advantage of this recourse—other codes more acceptably allowed a plaintiff's male guardian, or a chosen paladin, to duel the accused—but its existence attests at least principled judicial sentiment on behalf of women in the age of the Black Death.[14]

Particularly in property and criminal cases, women at law as a rule litigated through male representatives and beyond the swearing of an oath they did not have the right to speak on their own behalf in court. That requirement arose from circumstances beyond a woman's control, namely, her comparative lack of education and civic experience by comparison with the men she faced in court—a deficit that put her at a disadvantage in the medieval courtroom. Contemporaries deemed such male representation at law to be kind and protective, not misogynous, and some courts allowed a woman to choose her own spokeman rather than accept one appointed by her family or the court.[15]

There was, however, a major exception to the general rule of male representation at law: full-time businesswomen, single

or married, and wives who regularly engaged in their husbands'
trade. When disposing of property, swearing an oath, acting as
a witness, or standing as a defendant or a plaintiff in a civil or
criminal case, a working woman was generally recognized by
courts to be a fully legal person and thus capable of speaking
for herself. That concession acknowledged the professional
competence of working women and society's need to have all
business transactions legally binding, for otherwise those done
by women would remain beyond the reach of the law and disruptive of social order.[16] Although limitations continued to exist from place to place, and the privilege was more qualified in
some places than in others,[17] women who worked in a career or
a business outside the home enjoyed greater independence
within society and at law. This fact has led one historian to
praise the new career opportunities for women in the late Middle Ages as "a first foothold for woman's liberation from male
domination."[18]

Many historians believe that those opportunities did not
survive the sixteenth century, but fell victim to the changing
imperatives of a new industrial, commercial, and religious Europe. At the end of the fifteenth century, competition from the
countryside, where labor was plentiful and cheap, began to
close urban shops, particularly in the rapidly expanding print
and export trades. At the same time, the new commercial prominence of the Atlantic seaboard placed restraints on the growth

of central Europe's urban industries. In Germany, the new competition hit small workshops, where the businesses of women throve, hardest. Numerous shops survived only as suppliers of larger ones, and sizable numbers of women found themselves reduced to being low wage laborers in stagnating trades.[19] Forced to shift more of their labor to the home, women now produced on the premises a greater portion of the goods and services their families consumed.[20] By the end of the seventeenth century, women apprentices, who two centuries earlier held numerous secure jobs in guild industries, were apparently only a token presence in some.[21]

Whether the sixteenth century deserves the opprobrious titles "age of repression" and "epoch of despair" for women[22] is a question that cannot be answered until better head-counting has been done and more is known about the actual effects on contemporary women. Whether the changes alleged were truly unprecedented or only of degree remains unclear. It must also be asked whether sixteenth century women found their lives significantly diminished when careers went wanting in the trades. German historian Heide Wunder argues that the "return of women to the home" did not necessarily entail any great loss of self-worth, nor stifle their creative and productive capacities. In merchant and burgher households, women simply expanded their "home work," which was far more demanding than modern housewifery, consisting of routine gardening, slaughtering, cooking, making clothes, tutoring children, keeping family records, and assisting their husbands or fathers with the family business. At the same time, women at home developed new forms of "love work"—services for husband and children that kept hands busy and minds occupied, while enhancing the quality of family life for all.[23]

A positive commentary on the contemporary household may be derived from a little-noticed fact. The furious, organized resistance religious women are known to have offered when Protestant governments dissolved their cloisters and forced devout inmates back into parental homes and sometimes unwanted marriages[24] appears not to have found a counterpart on the secular labor front when women were squeezed out of urban handicraft and trade guilds. Perhaps the latter process was less disruptive because it developed slowly and was more subtle, and the women involved were not the sworn, eternal brides of Jesus Christ. The comparative calm on the secular labor front may also owe something to the challenges and satisfactions women continued to derive from the sixteenth century working household. As Heide Wunder has pointed out, "mere housewife" is a recent, not an old, pejorative.[25]

Women, Religion, and Society

Many studies maintain that it was not only economic forces that made the sixteenth century a fateful turning point in the history of working women. Contemporary politics and culture sanctioned equally fateful changes when society's inclination to keep women's reproductive and domestic roles primary gained support from newly centralized governments and compliant religious confessions willing to enshrine limited gender roles in secular law and Christian doctrine.[26]

If there is one issue on which a majority of modern historians agree, it is the detrimental effect of religion on the lives of women in the past: from the serial pregnancies and the restricted homemaking roles it decreed on the home front to the gender discrimination it sanctioned within the politics and the labor practices of public life. The Protestant Reformation and the Catholic Counter-Reformation are said to have left contemporary women only bit parts in the man's world outside the home. And entering marriages that were modeled on the "holy households" and "holy families" of the Bible, wives of both confessions could only play a subordinate role at home under the strict rule of their husbands.[27]

The new Lutheran family has particularly been stigmatized as "the prototype of the unconditionally patriarchal and authoritarian household" and "the nucleus" of the emerging totalitarian state.[28] Having demoted marriage from its traditional sacramental status, Martin Luther and his followers are said to have remanded it to the jurisdiction of the emerging Protestant state, where domestic life fell under greater scrutiny and harsher regulation than in Catholic lands.[29] That Martin Luther's domestic teaching should bear the brunt of such criticism is ironic, as even his detractors acknowledge his fierce criticism of antifeminist and antimarriage sentiment in the writings of ancient philosophers and the medieval clergy.[30] By sixteenth-century standards, Luther's wife, Katherina von Bora (1499–1552), a renegade nun, seems to have had it all. A homemaker and mother of six, she succeeded at several careers of her own choosing and making. After marrying the reformer, she improved their economic position by transforming the cells of the cloister that became their home into lodgings that could accommodate up to thirty paying students and guests. She profitably expanded its herb and vegetable gardens, gaining a reputation as a herbalist, and she purchased new land and vineyards, which she personally cultivated. She also repaired and operated the cloister brewery, producing beer good enough to be served at the Saxon elector's court.[31]

As the private and religious lives of people living in the centuries preceding the Reformation are more carefully studied, Luther and his followers are ceasing to be the first place historians turn to discover the social and economic forces shaping the modern destiny of women. Already in the later Middle Ages, that course had been charted by fundamental changes in European economies and societies, in light of which the role of religion in the story has become clearer and less malevolent. Only as caricatures of both principals can Protestant reformers be held responsible for the social changes in women's lives over the sixteenth century. Women and Protestantism were brought together in two novel developments, both well established in the previous century and embraced by both sides: the rise of marriage as the dominant lifestyle for adults and the movement of the family to the center of society-sustaining work and life.[32]

In the late Middle Ages, an unwanted circumstance—celibacy—had been the fate of untold thousands of propertyless freemen, clergy, and religious, who for economic and on religious reasons could never expect to marry, while the burghers and artisans who could and did marry often had to wait until their mid- to late twenties before being financially able to do so.[33] Urban governments at the time accommodated the predominant single lifestyle by creating brothels as an outlet for aggressive young males and a measure of protection from them for respectable young females, whose sexual purity was a key condition of success in the contemporary marriage market. Over the fifteenth century, however, marriage grew in popularity, spurred on by society's greater mobility, new economic opportunities, and heightened existential desire for companionship and family life after the decades of degradation caused by the great plague of the mid-fourteenth century.

Also exemplifying the new popularity of marriage at this time were the growing numbers of young adults exchanging private marriage vows without prior parental knowledge or consent. In an enterprising injection of itself into an emotionally charged domestic problem guaranteed to enhance its moral authority over family formation, the Church had pronounced "clandestine unions" based on the free consent of both partners to be true marriages in the eyes of God. Another development suggesting an urgent desire for marriage and family life was the growing number of clergy living openly in concubinage, not a few of them future Protestant pastors (Swiss reformer Ulrich Zwingli prominent among them). Increased litigation of those clandestine marriages and organized petitions and protests on the part of clergy wanting to marry legally further document the degree to which marriage had become a contender with the single life on the eve of the Reformation.[34]

The more favorable economic climate of the late fifteenth century meant that previously denied groups were now in a position to support a household, and to do so at earlier ages. Craft guilds eager to restrict admission to their ranks in the retrenching late-fifteenth-century urban labor markets also gave marriage a boost by making proof of legitimacy (that is, a documented parental marriage) a condition of apprenticeship. By century's end, the "celibacy-marriage-prostitution triad" that had previously organized gender relations to meet the needs of a society in which single people predominated was collapsing under these pressures. A new concept of marriage was needed, one around which family and society could reorganize to meet the imperatives of a changing domestic and commercial world.[35]

More than any other single force or institution, the Protestant Reformation supplied that new concept. From the start, the legalization of clerical marriage had been almost as fundamental a biblical tenet of the reformers as the sole authority of Scripture and the sufficiency of faith.[36] In the new theology, marriage became the lifestyle ordained by God and nature for all men and women with only the rarest exceptions (according to Luther, one in a thousand). Luther saw an ascending divine order of creation, running from family *(paterfamilias)* to state *(paterpoliticus)* to church *(patertheologicus)*. Indeed, "marriage pervades the whole of nature, for all creatures are divided into male and female; even trees marry; likewise, budding plants; there is also marriage between rocks and stones."[37]

From this point of view, it was a short, logical step to the closing of cloisters and brothels in the 1530s and 1540s in Protestant lands. The cloisters had already been shaken by centuries of clerical concubinage and sexual scandal, while the brothels—long a moral temptation for men while a moral shield for respectable young women—now posed a danger to society because of new syphilis epidemics. In a 1543 "Warning to Wittenberg Students" to avoid prostitutes—with whom students cavorted in the surrounding woods and on the banks of Wittenberg's fisheries—Martin Luther condemned prostitutes as "dreadful, shabby, stinking, loathsome, syphilitic people who can give their disease to ten, twenty, thirty, or more good people" over a few days' work: "Beware of whores and pray God to provide you with pious wives; you will have trouble enough as it is [in a proper marriage]."[38] In those same towns and territories, the creation of new lay-clerical marriage courts to replace the old episcopal ones gave reformers and magistrates alike a powerful new tool to rearrange and discipline domestic life in more effective and, Protestants believed, progressive ways.[39]

What the new clergy taught and preached about the relationship between the sexes they also attempted to exhibit in their own lives. In the footsteps of earlier, reform-minded humanists and Catholic clergy, Protestants took the lead in rejecting ancient and medieval portrayals of women as physically, mentally, and morally inferior to males.[40] While insisting on the husband's biblically commanded "headship," Lutherans praised intellectual cameraderie between husbands and wives and taught a pragmatic equality within marriage. Luther could respectfully call Katherina von Bora "Mr. Kathy" and describe his relationship with her thus: "I am an inferior lord, she the superior; I am Aaron, she is my Moses." The father of six children, he also ridiculed husbands who thought themselves above washing diapers and making beds alongside their wives.[41] Contrary to the customary testamentary practice of a husband's appointment of a male trustee or guardian to oversee his estate on behalf of his surviving widow and children, Luther made Katherina von Bora heir to all his modest property upon his death, confident that she would manage that property and care for their surviving children as well after his death as she had done before it.[42] Nowhere did such principled domestic equality in marriage find more consequential expression than in the legal innovation of Christian divorce and remarriage, which, while still rare and often taking years to complete in the sixteenth century, became a permanent legacy of Protestantism to the future equality of the sexes.[43]

In a popular marriage manual published in 1578, the Strasbourg poet and Lutheran Johann Fischart celebrated that still legally unequal, yet mutually respectful and functionally sharing, domestic partnership between husband and wife by comparing it to the relationship between the sun and the moon.[44] In earlier centuries, popes had famously invoked the same metaphor to declare the inferiority of the state to the Church and the emperor to the pope in a vain attempt to forestall secular aggression and maintain a degree of ecclesiastical hegemony, at least from the perspective of eternity.[45] Fischart's domestic turning of the phrase rather connoted the individuality and interdependence of husband and wife within the household, and also their moral equality and sharing of power. The sun may be larger and more radiant than the moon, yet the moon also has its rightful space and equal time— the two coexisting not in a static hierarchy of superordinate and subordinate, but rather in a cyclical process that perpetually validates each.[46]

From this perspective, some gender specialists reject the portrayal of European history since the fifteenth century as overwhelmingly a loss for women—what Heide Wunder describes as "the domestication of women through Luther, the driving of women out of the trades, and the persecution of women through witchhunts." Not only is it self-deceiving for modern scholars to expect "a general disappearance of social inequality and the hierarchy of marriage" in post-Renaissance Europe; it also sells contemporary women short when they are viewed as merely victims over centuries, and the gains that always accompany losses in changing societies are ignored.[47]

Not that there were no dark linings in those centuries. By the end of the Middle Ages, women wishing to learn a craft of their choice and work outside the home had more difficulty doing so. However, women who worked exclusively at home did not necessarily experience any great loss of self-worth nor find their creative and productive capacities stifled there.[48] Despite the drawbacks of marriage (frequent pregnancy, child rearing, deference to a husband), women of that time give every appearance of having preferred marriage and homemaking to living and working independently as domestics in the households of strangers and relatives. They seem also to have relished the authority they wielded as "housemothers," something renegade nuns claimed cloisters had no equivalent for, apart from a lucky few who became abbesses and prioresses. But then the latter, too, had to answer to supervisory, higher male clergy, who exercised the vital legal authority over cloisters and alone possessed the sacramental powers of priesthood, which were denied female heads of convents.[49]

Nor is there any substantial evidence that women at this time perceived themselves to be "professionless" and "childlike," or incapable of earning any money of their own, or being completely at the mercy of some all-providing, all-controlling paterfamilias. At marriage, the bride and bridegroom together furnished the wealth needed to establish a new household, and a wife continued to contribute her productive labor to that household. In addition, the professional training received at home by the wives and daughters of artisans and merchants engaged in family businesses often matched and might even exceed that available in a formal apprenticeship, putting home-trained women in a position—if and when they became widowed or otherwise found themselves on their own—to practice such skills independently.[50]

Married women's self-perception as co-workers and co-earners with their husbands can be seen in contemporary pamphlet and woodcut depictions of the "battle for the trousers," that is, over who wears the pants in the family.[51] The most domesticated women—the wives of lawyers, physicians, professors, and pastors—appear also to have been among the most confident of their position in marriage. Taking into account their dowries, the rental income they might continue to receive from family properties, the inheritances they looked forward to, and their own vital productivity within the household, these women contributed substantially to the material wealth of their new families. In addition, some of these women, like Katherina von Bora, became highly skilled at turning the raw products and land use with which their civil service husbands were sometimes paid into productive family assets.[52]

Another perceived dark lining for women in German lands was the sanctioning of the hierarchical ruling structure of the territorial state as a model for the organization of the household and the relationship between husband and wife.[53] Not only were camaraderie and sharing of household authority between spouses features of the new family order demanded by Lutheran reformers; so also, it is argued, were the twin hierarchies of state over household and of husband over wife. Those hierarchies were now inserted directly into family life by the same self-aggrandizing political regimes the reformers had initially embraced to secure their religious reforms.

Those who push this argument perceive new, government-sponsored family legislation manipulating the relationship between the sexes in two ways: first, by making marriage the only legitimate place for sex; and second, by enlisting spouses and parents in disciplinary tasks of government previously exercised by lords of manors and large communal households.[54] In the latter role, the husband is said to have become "the ruler's contact" on the home front,[55] the eyes and ears of the state and the Church within the household.

Unfortunately for this strained conspiratorial theory, but fortunately for the sixteenth-century family, the local politics of the household stubbornly resisted such political and ecclesiastical efforts to refashion the family into a mere cogwheel of state and Church. When a family extended itself into politics and religion, or received either's representatives or embraced either's goals within the household, what was foremost in mind was the usefulness of such connections to the success of family members in the outside world—not any desire to see the impersonal power of the state or of the Church encamped within the family circle itself.[56] For their part, the religious reformers cajoled princes and city councils as cleverly as rulers and governments managed the religious reforms—the enormous credulity of sixteeth-century rulers making them as amenable to the reformers' designs as the reformers' political vulnerablility made them to those of the rulers.[57]

The true scope of the shrinkage of women's vocational opportunities in urban trades and industry of the sixteenth century has yet to be empirically verified. It is clear, however, that it was not of such magnitude that women disappeared from the professional world beyond the home. Nor did the increase in women's productivity on the home front necessarily reduce them to mere housewives. When contemporary women departed the workplace and "returned" to the home, they took their restlessness and creativity with them. There, in the work of the sixteenth-century household, they found both old challenges and new opportunities while continuing to be in contact with the working world beyond.[58]

Although gender historians cannot yet be said to have discredited the cheery evolutionary scheme imposed on the early modern family by the historians of the 1960s and 1970s, their discovery of the prototype of the "modern" working woman in the labor markets of late medieval Europe should give any historian inclined to oversimply these matters pause. If women were so vital and prominent a part of the productive life of the fourteenth and fifteenth centuries, might they not reasonably be expected also to have found creative outlets for their talents in the changed labor markets of later centuries? A more promising women's history in these earlier centuries suggests the possibility of a more promising family history there as well. Although the historians of the 1960s and 1970s glimpsed the family of the past through the darkest of lenses, they also saw glimmers of light in the very century (the sixteenth) in which an incautious gender history would have us see only the twilight of womankind. If, as the one maintains, a brighter family history was dawning in the sixteenth century, might, as the other suggests, a more complex women's history also have been continuing from previous centuries?

❦ 3 ❧

REBUILDING THE
PREMODERN FAMILY

The compelling conclusion of the most recent research on the family is the difficulty of generalizing about it. Today, "low gradient affect" and "emotional isolation" are retreating pejoratives in informed family history, as are also wives who are "primarily baby machines," children who are not recognized as such, "hideously hurtful" child-rearing practices, "resolutely unerotic" teenagers, and hollow, mechanical households.

For the last two decades, the argument that a radical transformation occurred in family life between 1400 and 1800 has been on the chopping block, and the defining characteristics of the family, past and present, are again an open question. Today historians find alleged distinctive features of the "modern" family appearing from antiquity through the Renaissance; and, unlike the historians of the 1960s and 1970s, few blame the ills of present-day family life on the persistence of traditional family values.[1] For every historian who believes that the modern family is a recent, superior evolution, there is another who is ready to expose it as a fallen archetype. And while the one worries that today's family cannot survive its seemingly endless reconfigurations, the other points to the great variety of single-parent, blended, and nonhierarchical families populating the distant past—products then of a mercilessly high mortality rate rather than rampant elective divorce and voluntary lifestyle changes.

The most important question to be asked of the family is whether it has bedrock. Is there something upon which families have built in every age and onto which they may safely collapse if and when their ever-changing societies and cultures fail them—a "family within the family," so to speak?

Antiquity

As a rule, the farther back in time one goes, the fewer, more indirect, and less personal the sources for family history become. Still, much credible information has been wrung from the most distant sources. In addition to the family's physical traces in the environment of everyday life, from linens to latrines, the family has remained a prominent subject of administrative and court proceedings, legal codes, wills, tax records, art, literature, medical writings, sermons, advice books, proverbs, and songs.[2] In second-century Rome, legal codes indicate that marriage had ceased to be a total merger of a wife with her husband's family. New laws, instigated by concerned parents, placed limits on male guardianship and recognized the maturity of both partners and their respective property rights. The new Roman marriage treated a new family as a "separate regime" with dual origins, matrilineal and patrilineal, woman's history as well as man's.[3] The bridegroom now reciprocated the bride's dowry with a wedding gift of his own (the brideswealth), which thereafter became the property of the wife. A wife could now repossess the property and wealth she brought into a marriage upon her husband's death or their divorce (the latter at either's initiative), while the husband was held accountable for his stewardship of that property and wealth. Literary evidence suggests that marriages among both elite (patrician) and nonelite (soldiers and slaves) could be loyal and loving.[4]

By the later Roman Empire (fourth century), women pursued careers, supported themselves, and delayed marriage, sometimes even avoiding it altogether. Behind this development lay no ancient feminism, although a kind of "feminist critique" of marriage by celibate male clergy, who portrayed it as totally burdensome for both sexes, may have contributed to it. The immediate cause of this expansion of careers outside the home—as would be the case again and again in subsequent centuries—was a dire shortage of male workers, in this instance, due to acute depopulation. Contributing to this depopulation was an odd tandem of pagan and Christian moralists—the former by recommending the single life, contraception, abortion, and the exposure of unwanted children, the latter by praising celibacy, virginity, and continence.[5]

The Middle Ages

By the eleventh and twelfth centuries, some of the equity in marriage achieved in late antiquity and preserved throughout the early Germanic Middle Ages began to be reversed by a resurgence of paternal authority. The brideswealth that endowed women with property and power of their own now fell out of fashion, while the bride's dowry remained. At the same time new practices of patrilineage and primogeniture awarded family property and wealth to favored males as disproportionately as ever.[6]

Historians, however, still find evidence of sexy, companionate marriages and sentimental families at the higher social levels of this reputedly dawning dark age in the relationship between the sexes (1000–1200). From popular troubadour music and poetry to the chronicles and correspondence of the elite, anecdotal and literary evidence suggests the existence of full and satisfying emotional lives in the High Middle Ages.[7]

The sentimentality of the medieval family has also been infered from surviving saints' lives and miracle stories. Describing the households and familial relationships in which candidates for sainthood grew up, these works evoke contemporary representations of motherhood, fatherhood, and childhood that belie portrayals of medieval society as antimarriage and antifamily and those of the medieval family as an "emotional desert."[8]

Because different social groups did not have the same work requirements, families in the distant past organized their households and activities in different ways—some in directions that have been described as "transitional" or "modernizing." As a general rule, all household members remained subordinate to the paterfamilias, whose strong leadership was deemed essential to household unity, security, and success. However, a wife might have greater or lesser freedom and responsibility depending on the requirements of a particular household. Because virtually every facet of household management required the attention and input of the peasant wife, patriarchy has been found to be weakest among the underclasses and the peasant household the least inclined to divide chores along strict gender lines.[9]

At the other end of the social spectrum, the noble wife was the most isolated and restricted, especially if she lived in one of medieval Germany's 5,000 remote castles. Unlike her burgher counterpart in the cities, who shared the legal protections and privileges of citizenship with her husband and could take a direct role in his business, the castle wife often lived alone in a comparatively isolated fortress, her fair treatment guaranteed only by the marriage contract between two, often distant, families.[10]

Contraception

Another marker of the modern family for which evidence is found in much earlier centuries is the practice of contraception. Ariès believed it gained currency in the eighteenth century "just when the family finished organizing itself around the child and raised the wall of private life between [itself] and society."[11] Flandrin agreed, but viewed its appearance ironically, as an unintended consequence of Christian moral teaching, not an original product of the new secular world of the Enlightenment.[12] But if this thesis is true, why had not Church teaching had such an effect much earlier, when (1) spousal and parental dilemmas traceable to outsized families were arguably more pressing, and (2) the New Testament commandment to love one's neighbor as oneself was no less prominent in the Church's teaching than the Old Testament commandment to be fruitful and multiply?

At first glance, contraception in the Middle Ages may seem an oxymoron. Not only had the Church condemned it early in its history,[13] nonprocreative sex was the last thing newlyweds desired, and couples as a rule were not done with childbearing until a sizable family existed as a hedge against high mortality. Once married, women in all social classes looked on sterility as the greatest curse of a marriage and pursued remedies against it as if they were golden.[14] Religious women also embraced the roles of spiritual wives and mothers rather than that of independent single women, and they did so to extreme. Not only did they become the brides of Christ, they were the most abject and subservient of brides, seeking through utter self-denial and self-sacrifice to merge their own mind, will, and desire completely with those of their Bridegoom. These women also became the most tender and indulgent of mothers. Having as a rule received a Christ-child doll of their own upon entrance, many a cloistered girl or young woman had visions of baby Jesus and spiritual birth fantasies, becoming in their own way "mothers of God."[15]

How could a contraceptive mentality develop in a culture so maternal that even those who most emphatically denied marriage and motherhood replicated these states in their daily activities and contemplations? The case for "appreciable contraception" in the Middle Ages is based on church records, eyewitness reports of clergy in regular contact with laity, and demographic data. Church records document a great variety of contraceptive devices in use by the laity: simple abstinence, herbal tinctures and acidic ointments, sponges, oral sex, mutual masturbation, sodomy, prolonged nursing of infants, postponement of marriage (complex abstinence?), and coitus interruptus, the contraceptive practice most frequently confessed by married couples.[16] Saint Catherine of Siena (1347–1380), who was her parents' twentieth child, condemned contraception as the "most frequent" sin of married people and the one contemporary parents were least contrite about—an observation also frequently made by late medieval preachers.[17] Beyond such anecdotal evidence, studies comparing the ages of women at first marriage and the number of children they subsequently bore have found that women marrying in their thirties frequently had just as many children as those who married between fifteen and twenty-five—a circumstance that only the practice of birth control would seem to explain.[18]

While decreeing marriage to be the only legitimate place for sexual relations, and the production of offspring their sole justification, medieval Church dogma also recognized companionship and mutual sharing of affection as grounds for marriage. Significantly, it did not, however, deem sexual relations necessary for the full realization of affection. In training manuals for priests, theologians taught a distinction between sex for the purpose of progeny (morally good) and sex only for carnal pleasure (morally bad).[19] If, as some argue, Christian teaching ironically encouraged a contraceptive mentality among the laity, it may more readily have come by way of this emphatic distinction rather than through any suddenly transforming, internalized Christian ethic of love, such as that Flandrin saw "maturing" over the seventeenth and eighteenth centuries. When confronted by the "sin of contraception" at confession, married parishioners were in a far stronger position than their priests to appreciate the distinction in sexual purpose. As sexually experienced adults, they would have understood well that satisfying, guiltless sex might occur and a good marriage exist without any conscious desire for offspring during sexual relations. From this point of view, the priests who harped on this distinction may have stiffened the resolve of ordinary people to keep the pleasure of sex while foregoing unwanted or too-frequent pregnancies by the best contraceptive means available.

In church records from the thirteenth and fourteenth centuries, the laity offered the following justifications for what, to their clergy's mind, was immoral contraceptive practice: to avoid the pain of childbirth, escape impoverishment, preserve health and beauty, and prolong sexual intercourse for a longer period of time before a new pregnancy interrupted it—reasons suggesting that couples found sex pleasurable, eagerly pursued it, pondered its consequences for themselves and their offspring, and discussed contraceptive options. For their part, priests respected only impoverishment as a motive, and some may have shown leniency to couples who violated Church law on such grounds by assigning lighter penances. In secular law, impoverishment was also the only legal defense that could save a woman convicted of infanticide from summary execution.[20]

❧ 4 ❧

THE OMNIPRESENT CHILD

Along-standing consensus has held that a child's lot in life is always more precarious than that of a wife, and not a few scholars of the family today would agree with American psychohistorian Lloyd DeMause's famous declaration in 1974 that "the history of childhood is a nightmare from which we have only recently begun to awaken." Convinced that the treatment of children had become progressively competent and kinder with the passage of centuries, DeMause went so far as to postulate six "improving modes of parent-child relations" in human history, beginning in antiquity, when infanticide is said to have typified parent-child relations, and culminating in the mid-twentieth century when, allegedly for the first time, "helpfulness" became the dominant parental attitude toward children.[1]

Such somber assessments of childhood in the past reappear today particularly when family historians confront Protestant parents, whose basic child-rearing practices are said to derive from malevolent biblical belief in original sin and human depravity. In a recent survey of historical research on children and childhood since 1500, Hugh Cunningham describes the Protestant family as "a microcosm of [both] the church and the state" and a nursery devoted to training the young for service in each. Despite that research's confirmation of progressive equality between spouses, Cunningham reads the evidence on children to be far more ambiguous. Yes, Ariès was wrong to say that parents in the past did not recognize distinct stages of childhood and treated their children as little adults. Still, the arrival of children in the household, especially Protestant households, is said to have created as much anxiety as joy for parents, who resolved their frustration by subordinating their children "for the sake of their salvation."[2]

The scholarly perception of stifled children, particularly in Protestant homes, parallels that of stifled wives, also especially to be found in the "holy households" of Protestants. In neither case, however, is the evidence watertight. Cunningham's survey takes no account of the ground-breaking microhistorical studies of German childhood and youth written during the 1980s and 1990s.[3] And his penchant for interpreting family life through abstract religious dogmas, rather than through first-person accounts by the subjects themselves in surviving family archives, leaves his conclusions on this subject partial and wobbly.[4]

Despite the persistence of such questionable judgments on the parents of the past, twenty-five years of new research since DeMause's famous essay have produced a flood of scholarship contesting their fairness and accuracy. Today, parental awareness that childhood has its own distinct ages and stages, special needs and vulnerabilities, has been documented all the way back to antiquity. While the subjects of these historical investigations have professed different religious faiths, loving parents and well-recognized children have been identified in them all. By contrast, no credible study to date has documented at the grass roots of any society or religious confession a pervasive parental inability to recognize and enter a child's world, or to treat children caringly. Nor does one readily discover families and households that view themselves primarily as outposts for state and church. To the contrary, the ability of ancient and medieval authorities to schematize and value childhood compares well with that of modern pediatric experts. Jean Piaget's four flexible stages of childhood (infancy, early childhood, middle childhood, and adolescence) and Erik Erikson's five more specific ones (infancy, early childhood, the age of play, school age, and youth) are not so different from those of early medieval authorities such as Fulgentius of Ruspe (active ca. 484–496) and Isidore of Seville (ca. 570–636).[5] Indeed, the critical historian of these early centuries may well wonder whether our modern experts have been unknowing plagiarizers.

Fulgentius, for example, described birth and early childhood as a time when infants discover their physical abilities and rudimentary cognitive skills. Although able to see, infants cannot recognize the objects in the world around them, including their mothers, and, lacking the power of speech, they must obtain what they want by crying. What they most like to do, Fulgentius observed, is to nurse at their mother's breast and be sung to by her.[6] In his *Etymologies*, an authoritative medieval textbook, Isidore distinguished four preadult stages of life: early childhood (*infantia*, birth to seven), boyhood and girlhood (*pueritia*, seven to twelve for girls and up to fourteen for boys), early adolescence (*adolescentia*, or the "growing up" years, fourteen into the early twenties), and postadolescence (*iuventus*, or the "flowering" years, from the late teens to the late twenties).[7]

The more specific pediatric literature of antiquity and the Middle Ages broke childhood into three separate phases, end-ing in the late teens: infancy proper (birth to first teeth and weaning, occurring as early as seven months or as late as two years); "second infancy" (two to seven); and boyhood and girl-hood (seven to at least fourteen and as late as seventeen). Roman law placed youths under adult guardianship in civil matters until they were twenty-five, and the Church withheld the full adult penalties for sexual and other sins until a person reached twenty, although boys and girls did penance for such behavior at fourteen and twelve years respectively.[8]

Investment in Children

If there is a turning point in parent-child relations, when the treatment of children appears to have improved, many today would see it occurring in the four centuries between 1100 and 1500, roughly the same period in which gender historians find expanding vocational opportunities for working women. Three developments are associated with the betterment of children: the growing affluence of cities; the increasing success of the Church's moral teaching; and the revival of classical educational models stressing patience and persuasion in child rearing.[9]

Although lacking a critical mass of sources, scholars of earlier medieval centuries have also documented the recognition of children. From the observations and recollections of family life left by the clergy and religious, it has been argued that parents as early as the ninth century knew the difference between treatment that was psychologically harmful and that which fostered a child's sense of well-being. Alongside the ancient proprietary notion of children as the chattel of their parents, clerical commentators repeatedly observed an "awakening of parental conscience" to the neglect, exploitation, and abandonment of children.[10]

Both saints' lives and the popular cult of the Christ child—the latter emerging from the Cistercian order in the twelfth century—portray caring mothers and fathers on the model of Mary and Joseph, while less subjective sources document Christian Europe's social and psychological investment in children between the twelfth and fifteenth centuries. In great cities like Florence and Rome, that investment can be quantitatively measured in the growing number of urban schools, orphanages, and hospitals; increased vocational training and opportunities for the young; and new attention paid to children's health and hygiene.[11]

Anecdotal evidence of parental sentiment is often striking and everywhere to be found in the distant past. In a century when a third or more of all children died by their early teens from disease or accident, a twelfth-century church column in Vézelay portrays a grief-stricken father placing a tightly bundled dead child at the feet of St. Benedict in the hope of its revival[12]—a scene reenacted many times during the annual pilgrimages of the Middle Ages, which drew parents with ailing children to the shrines of the Virgin and the Church's lesser saints in the hope of a miraculous cure.[13]

In late medieval and Renaissance Europe, stillborn children were named, lamented, buried, and counted by their parents in family genealogies along with their surviving siblings.[14] Well-to-do families chiseled not only their coats of arms and genealogies on the gravestones of deceased children, but also the likenesses of the dogs and birds the children had loved and played with in life.[15]

Family archives document both the professed greatest fears of newlyweds (sterility, miscarriage, stillbirth, and the death of an unbaptized newborn) and the greatest joys of new parents (playing with, nursing, diapering, and washing the newborn). From quickening to adulthood, the major passages and traumas of children were noted. There was the first kick in the womb, the baptism and naming, and the first unassisted steps (the last might occur in well-to-do families after weeks of practice with a walker and the protection of a leather cap). There was the ordeal of teething, which might be assisted by draping unhappy infants with necklaces of wolf or horse teeth, or the severed, dried feet of a leapfrog—extreme measures by hapless parents to evoke stalled teeth. Parents also remembered a child's first distinct words, first fancy dress or suit of clothes, and—the most ambivalent of all parental experiences—a child's departure from home for apprenticeship, service, or schooling.[16]

A striking story of emotional parental involvement with children appears in the St. Gall chronicle of Johannes Kessler (1502/1503–1574), who in an entry for 1536 recorded the mauling death of a local boy by a supposedly tame bear. The bear was kept by its owners in a shed behind the town granary, where it performed for crowds on special occasions. The unfortunate boy had apparently carelessly entered the shed. When the news hit the streets of St. Gall, a general panic ensued because, as Kessler explained, many parents did not have their sons immediately at their sides, and thus feared that the slain boy might be their own.[17] Kessler himself, needlessly as it turned out, also panicked, as he had just sent his son Joshua home along a route that took him past the granary.

Against all such evidence of loving parents, modern skeptics allege three discretionary cruelties to infants said to have been frequently practiced by parents in the past: infanticide, swaddling, and wet-nursing.

Infanticide

Numerous reports of the accidental death of infants and children raise a reasonable suspicion of criminal negligence and premeditated murder by uncaring or impoverished parents wanting to limit the size of their families and by single women trying to escape the stigma and penalties of unwed motherhood. Such suspicions have particularly been raised in the case of female offspring, whose numbers are underrepresented in not a few contemporary censuses.[18]

Recognizing that too many unwanted children could move poor parents to contraception and infanticide, the Church acted early to discourage both. As early as the sixth century, priests warned mothers not to sleep with newborns and infants, and subjected those who lost children to alleged accidental smothering *(oppressio infantium)* to stiff penances. Church synods later forbade new mothers and wet nurses from taking infants and small children into their beds, and parents of children who accidentally drowned, burned, or fell to their deaths could expect at the very least to do penance for negligence.[19]

Wherever the Church had a commanding presence, it projected a model family life in the form of the Holy Family: a loving mother (Mary) nursing and caring for her son and a loyal father (Joseph) utterly devoted to both, even though he had not sired his son.[20] The foundling homes co-sponsored by the Church and city governments reported few deaths from negligence or improper care—a fitting response, if accurate, as those homes became in the thirteenth century society's first line of defense against infanticide and child abandonment, when the moral teaching of the Church and the draconian laws of the state failed to deter unwanted and out-of-wedlock births.[21]

A less drastic explanation than female infanticide also exists for the gender disparity in censuses. The medieval census-taker all too naturally focused on male heads of households, probably counting some wives with their husbands and taking greater notice of male heirs than of their sisters.[22] Gender prejudice, not gendercide, may be the more reasonable explanation for much undercounting. In some places, all the relevant records point away from premeditated infanticide. Late-fifteenth- and early-sixteenth-century London had fewer than one allegation per year, and none produced a conviction.[23] The hard evidence for infanticide in medieval and Renaissance Europe comes from criminal behavior typical of every age and not from any documented popular belief that exposing newborns was an accepted means of family planning. When gross per capita statistics for infanticide, child abuse, and violence against women in the Middle Ages are compared to those for present-day Europe and the United States, the results have suggested that the modern world has far more sins to atone for than the premodern.[24]

When addressing the subject of child abuse in the past, family historians of the 1980s and 1990s have been far less inclined to rely on the social sciences than were those of the 1960s and 1970s. The former warn against substituting models and theories derived from present-day clinical or field studies for microhistorical analysis of historical periods within an authentic contemporary framework. Psychologist Erik Erikson, for example, could confidently interpret the lives of sixteenth-century German reformer Martin Luther (1962) and nineteenth- and twentieth-century Hindu nationalist Mahatma Gandhi (1969) with the same theory of human developmment derived from his clinical studies of twentieth-century gifted youth.[25] The consequences of such approaches to the past, historians fear, may be a dubious projection of modern values and conflicts onto a premodern world incorrectly assumed to have been as dysfunctional or crisis-ridden as our own, and for much the same reasons.[26]

As every good detective knows, consequences can shed light on their antecedents. However, since history develops from earlier to later centuries, and only a preceding century can shed light on one that follows, there is always a danger of overriding the true preoccupations of an earlier age when it is approached, as much modern historical study is inclined to do, with an eye only to determining where that age stands on some burning present-day issue. But the historically informed work of anthropologist William Christian, Jr., and the anthropologically sophisticated historical work of Natalie Zemon Davis suggest that, in the hands of true experts, historical research and the social sciences can work hand in hand without the one surrendering abjectly to the other or egregiously distorting the past.[27]

Child-rearing practices that appear to be backward and cruel under modern conditions actually made good sense and succeeded under the different conditions of an earlier age. A rural mother in northern Europe during the Middle Ages had good reason, beyond infanticide, for taking a newborn or an infant into a crowded communal family bed. Doing so prevented the child from freezing to death in winter and being mauled by household or straying animals year-round; furthermore, in a great many premodern households there was no other place for an infant or child to sleep. That some suffocated under such conditions, and criminal parents intentionally smothered others, proves neither widespread infanticide nor, much less, any tacit societal approval of it.[28]

Swaddling

Swaddling is another alleged example of incompetent and uncaring parenting in the past, and while both anecdotal literary and medical evidence indicate that infants were left to stew in their urine and feces for long periods of time,[29] such neglect was also neither a universal practice nor condoned by contemporary authorities. In late medieval Nürnberg, stacks of diapers or swaddling were standard gifts for new mothers, and burgher parents prided themselves on not leaving their children long in soiled swaddling.[30] Frankfurt city physician Eucharius Rösslin, author of the leading lay guide to pregnancy and early child care (*Der Rosengarten*, 1513), recommended changing and bathing infants several times a day, as did Johannes Coler in his great "housefather book" (1594), a guide to household management that instructed parents to allow infants to kick freely on a pillow during the day and not remain always diapered.[31]

If the instruction of the medieval pediatrician "gently to swaddle" seems an oxymoron to modern critics, it was both a kindness and a prophylaxis for contemporary infants living in the leaky and insecure houses of the Middle Ages. A swaddled infant was more easily carried about by mothers busy at their chores, and contemporaries believed that swaddling instilled a feeling of security in an infant and helped its limbs grow straight and shapely. Still today, at the end of the twentieth century, physicians recommend swaddling as a way to calm colicky infants. For contemporary moralists, it had the further benefit of inhibiting the animalistic behavior of crawling about on all fours, too much of which was thought to stimulate premature development of a child's bestial nature.[32]

Wet-Nursing

Wet-nursing is another scorned medieval practice being reevaluated today. For noble and well-to-do burgher mothers, hiring a wet nurse to suckle a newborn was both an act of conspicuous consumption and an escape from the physical inconveniences nursing was known to cause (sleeplessness, raw or infected nipples, physical disfigurement, and a longer confinement). For parents eager to have additional progeny, the contraceptive effect of maternal nursing made it undesirable, and nursing mothers could also become torn between their conjugal and their maternal duties, as they knew that a quick pregnancy imperiled their milk supply. However, physicians and clergy continued to insist on the health benefits of mother's milk, and most new mothers agreed. Wet-nursing was popular only among a small minority of the upper classes, probably never more than 4 percent of the overall population of nursing mothers at any time.[33]

Before pasteurization made bovine and goat's milk completely safe to drink, parents feared a diet of animal milk in the first months of life far more than they did that of an alien nurse. The Basel printer Thomas Platter (1507?–1582), who was a sickly child and suffered poor health as an adult, blamed both conditions on the goat's milk he was fed throughout infancy (through a cow's horn), after his mother's milk supply failed.[34] Because wet-nursing was the prefered alternative when a mother could not nurse, women of all social classes might have occasion to seek such services. Weaning from human milk ordinarily began by a child's first birthday and was completed within six months. However, premodern parents, always looking ahead in a child's life, varied a child's liquid diet much earlier. There are examples of diluted bovine or goat's milk, along with diluted beer and wine, supplementing a child's liquid diet as early as four months.[35]

As a purely discretionary practice, wet-nursing was more popular in some lands and cultures than in others. In parts of late medieval Italy, the urban middle classes appear to have put newborns out to wet nurses almost as routinely as nobility and royalty.[36] By contrast, wet-nursing was minimal or nonexistent in medieval London.[37] And among the patrician and upper burgher classes of late medieval Nürnberg, mothers with few exceptions nursed their own newborns; those who did not, as a rule, brought the nurse into their own homes rather than send their infants out to hers.[38] Such "nursing-in" benefited both the hiring family's newborn and the nonnursing mother, although not always the nurse herself. If she were a recent widow without a nursling, having either lost an infant of her own or recently weaned one, her unhappy situation made her ideal for the hiring parents, for she then could easily live in and devote all of her attention and milk supply to their newborn.[39]

Play

Two views of child rearing held sway between 1400 and 1600; one was said to be more medieval and German, the other closer to the spirit of the Italian Renaissance, although both are found in each land and culture.[40] Each viewed a child as basically unformed at birth. According to the first, the key to a child's development lay in its imitative nature: children, like monkeys, adapted to the environment in which they were placed and realized their adult selves by internalizing the behavior, skills, and virtues they saw around them in others.[41] The second view stressed the individuality of the child over a malleable generic nature, portraying every child as having its own inborn talent, which interaction with others elicited. From both points of view, the more varied a child's early experience, the steadier and truer its development would be.

Both points of view accommodated the Judeo-Christian belief in the fall of Adam and Eve and its effect on human nature, which encouraged devout educators and parents to pursue a highly structured and religious upbringing for children at home and at school.[42] And both also encouraged parents to socialize their children at an early age by placing them in the company of others. In 1532, at only two months, baby Georg Scheurl's tiny hand was guided by his famous father—then Nürnberg's lead lawyer and diplomat—as the boy wrote thank-you notes and letters of greeting to the important people in his father's present and his own future world. As Georg and his brother grew, their father brought playmates who represented

Nürnberg's social spectrum, from artisans to royalty, into their nursery in an attempt to prepare them early for the world they would enter as adolescents and adults. [43]

Reigning contemporary theories of child development also recommended patient adaptation as a more effective parental strategy than coercion of children in directions they did not go easily. To this extent, both philosophies minimized corporal punishment (always to be a last resort) and gave teenagers and young adults a role in choosing among the vocational options realistically available to them.[44] While modern scholars tend to associate such constructive approaches to child rearing with classical authors and give the humanist revival of antiquity very generous credit for them,[45] none of this would have escaped ordinary parental observation and trial and error. The same assumptions about child nature and development put children at tender ages (between eight and fourteen, depending on social class and career) in service, apprenticeship, and school outside the home while giving privileged patrician and burgher youths the opportunity to complete their maturation and education by traveling widely from land to land and university to university during their mid-teens and early twenties.

Infants, toddlers, teenagers, and adolescents abounded in the distant past, their relics and markings everywhere to be found, documenting a child's world back to antiquity: rattles, clay and paper dolls, wheeled horses and wagons, sleds, balls, stilts, even miniature gardening tools. Surviving illustrations depict boys and girls playing marbles, shooting dice, jumping rope, flying kites, dragging tame birds and reluctant beetles about on strings, spinning tops, rolling hoops, puffing into blowguns, and riding stick horses while pinwheels spin in their free hand. Between the twelfth and fourteenth centuries, noble and patrician boys staged tournaments with puppet knights and horsemen. Elaborate doll houses and massive boxed gardens costing thousands of gulden were the toys of the children of late medieval Germany's very rich. On Christmas Day 1572 elector August of Saxony gave his then twelve-year-old son and future successor an entire and apparently life-size toy hunt: four pairs each of stags, hinds, roe-deer, boars, foxes, wolves, and rabbits, twenty-four dogs, six hunters on foot and seven on horseback, to which ten horses, a mule, and a sleigh were added, each professionally crafted from the best materials.[46]

Favorite group games were ball, ring-around-the-roses, hide-and-go-seek, forfeits, chase, blind cow, thieves and sheriffs, musical chairs, and freeze. Children also liked to pretend to be animals (particularly horses and goats) and to imitate their parents. In winter, snowballs, snowmen, sleds, and ice skating filled the short days, while fairy tales, riddles, and tongue-twisters ("Fred Fischer feasted on fresh fish") helped pass the long, cold, dark nights.[47] During the annual civic and religious festivals, children were given prominent roles. On Palm Sunday, palm branches in hand, they led, rode, or accompanied the symbolic donkey on which Christ had entered Jerusalem. For the popular school festival of Saint Gregory the Great, celebrated on March 12 in the warmer south and in late May in the colder north, a child was chosen bishop and two of his mates priests; together they would enter the church in clerical dress to preach their own sermons to peers and elders. On Trinity, the first Sunday after Pentecost, two patrician boys led the annual Corpus Christi parade in Nürnberg, strewing roses in its path, while in Frankfurt am Main, three hundred boys, dressed in white and carrying white candles, escorted the Holy Eucharist through the streets. At the start of spring, children staged a mock battle against winter (death), which was represented by a straw man, whom the children surrounded, trampled, and burned or buried—or, in towns like Nürnberg, which had rivers running through them, unceremoniously drowned.[48]

The feasts of Saint Martin (November 11), Saint Nicholas (December 6), New Year's, and Epiphany (January 6) were gift days for children, on which they received candy and pastries, new clothes, silver spoons, and gold and silver coins. Nürnberg's annual "Christ Child Market" turned the city into one of Europe's grandest toy stores. At Carnival or Shrovetide, masked children went from house to house begging treats and joining in the irreverent role reversals that marked pre-Lenten celebrations. In some places, they awakened their parents rudely with fir or birch switches (the standard instrument of corporal punishment), lifting the siege only after being promised pancakes or pretzels.[49]

Work

Preparing a child to live and work independently was a parent's highest duty and chief obsession. To that end, fathers held greater legal authority over offspring than did mothers, and that authority continued to be exercised until children entered their majority (between eighteen and twenty-five) and were in a position to marry and support a household on their own.[50] Despite considerable sharing of parental responsibility during the first five years of a child's life, the day-to-day rearing of boys and girls was largely in a mother's hands. At six or seven, however, a son made the passage "from smock to trousers," shedding the dress previously worn by both sexes and donning the pants of male authority,[51] henceforth increasingly to be directed into the father's world.

Although gender now increasingly controlled vocational destiny and parental attention, mothers remained involved in the rearing of their sons, as did fathers in that of their daughters. After a father's death, the widowed burgher mother, in concert with appointed male guardians, might take the lead role *in loco patris,* directing the lives of both minor sons still at home and adolescent and young adult sons away at school or in apprenticeships. Widowed fathers were no less active on their daughters' behalf.[52]

Six or seven was also an important age for children in civil and church law. The major south German law codes did not hold children younger than seven responsible for their actions *(strafunmündig)* and exempted them from adult legal prosecution and punishment.[53] For the Church, seven was the earliest age at which a child might knowingly commit a mortal sin; and until the young reached the canonical ages of physical maturity (twelve for girls and fourteen for boys), the Church went easier on them, simplifying confessions and giving lighter penances to match.[54] Lutherans, however, believed that the "sleep of reason" (a child's years of relative innocence) ended around the age of five.[55]

No more than the Church did parents and society yank children out of childhood at six or seven and subject them to adult expectations and rules. The goal of parenting was indeed a "passive" child, but for contemporaries that meant a child docile enough to obey and hence to learn, so that he or she might in turn also be able to resist and thus to survive the temptations of a dangerous world.[56] With these dialectical but complementary goals in mind, a mean between leniency and severity became the disciplinary ideal. A properly raised child was neither indulged nor punished too little or too much.[57]

If, however, a choice had to be made, contemporaries deemed the overzealous parent less blameworthy than the indifferent one, agreeing that "he who spares the rod hates his son, but he who loves him is diligent to discipline him" (Proverbs 13:24). A truism for premodern parents, that bit of biblical analysis has also become a rod with which modern critics have beaten them as well: here, in a phrase, is said to be the bitter fruit of the cleric's misanthropic belief in original sin and resentful parents' revenge on their offspring for having been themselves denied self-determination in their own childhoods.[58]

Having completed their private study at home and local public schooling by twelve or thirteen, most children entered service, apprenticeship, or higher education outside the parental home.[59] Boys began merchant apprenticeships between twelve and sixteen, spending four to six years mastering their skills. Those destined for university study and professional careers in law and government enrolled between thirteen and seventeen, just before their sisters became eligible for marriage (sixteen or seventeen) and contemplated future moves of their own into a husband's household; or, lacking a proper marriage, into lifelong domestic service in a relative's or neighbor's household or posssibly entry into a cloister. By contrast, artisan youth destined for the trades might apprentice out as early as seven or eight, although the norm was between ten and twelve. Their training could continue into their early twenties, although, like their patrician and burgher counterparts in merchant apprenticeships, the trade apprenticeship normally lasted four to six years.[60]

Few contemporary parents had any qualms about a system that took children away from home at young ages, nor did they doubt its effectiveness in realizing the goals they set early in life for their children. The sadness of separation and the foreseen difficulties of life in new households with new masters were not allowed to lessen the importance of this occasion. A child's ability to leave home and prepare for an independent adult life, henceforth to be useful to self and to others, had been the parents' goal for their offspring since the day of the child's birth. Separation was a logical continuation of a process that had begun at home, not a dreaded, cruel break or the dissolution of the family.[61]

A Peasant Couple Going Off to a Dance by Hans Weiditz (1521)

The comparatively greater sharing of farm work by both sexes—women's hands being needed and welcomed in the barn and in the fields as well as at the hearth—may have contributed to greater comfort, equality, and happiness between farming men and women. The caption accompanying this romanticized portrayal of peasant life reads:

> How blessed is the farmer,
> Who can feed himself with a plough.
> While the troubled rich man tosses and turns,
> He sleeps in peace on either side.
> The water jug's enough for him,
> And he is not distracted by quarrels of the heart.
> A more devout people have not been born.
> Of their failings disloyalty is the least.

From Max Geisberg, *The German Single-Leaf Woodcut, 1500–1550*, vol. 4, ed. Walter L. Strauss (New York: Hacker Art Books, 1974), p. 1478. By permission of Abaris Books.

Creating an Orderly Household by Hans Sachs and
Hans Guldenmund (ca. 1530)

Battering husbands and shrewish wives were exceptions in premodern society, not the norm. Neither was respected, much less encouraged, by law, custom, state, or church. When abusive marriages did occur, the husband, as head of household, received the lion's share of blame. The result in popular didactic literature was both a plea for greater gender equality and a wink at continuing sexism.

A fictional story of a shaky new marriage accompanies this depiction of marital strife. As confessed by the bruised husband to a happily married friend, the fight began when he struck his new wife for refusing to speak to him after he returned home from a night of drinking. "Unacceptable hot-tempered, petulant, mad, stupid, shameless behavior," his friend exclaimed—not on her part but on *his!* An orderly household is to be created by peace and friendship, not by war. "As St. Paul says, we men should rule our wives with reasonable words and not harass and crudely tyrannize them." By "alternating sweet and sour," the couple is said to have their best chance to become, in time, of one mind. From Max Geisberg, *The German Single-Leaf Woodcut, 1500–1550,* vol. 1, ed. Walter L. Strauss (New York: Hacker Art Books, 1974), p. 137. By permission of Abaris Books.

The Subjugated Male by Israhel von Meckenem (ca. 1480–1490)

Contrary to the presumed divine order of male-female and husband-wife relations, the wife here portrayed has succeeded in turning her household upside down. She has usurped the authority that properly belongs to her husband and now mean-spiritedly abuses it. As he sits in her place at the loom, unwinding a spindle of wool with a wary eye, she pulls on the male underpants *(brouch)* typical of the fifteenth and sixteenth centuries and threatens him with the distaff. Spurning the submissive, cooperative biblical role of a helpmate, she has become a scold and he, much worse for the times, a defeated male and failed husband. By permission of the Graphische Sammlung Albertina, Vienna.

Women Bathing by Hans Sebald Beham, 1540

The premodern world, like the modern, was both curious and proper, full of desire as well as piety. A case in point is the public bath, which men and women shared, attending at different times of the day or on alternate days. Bathroom rendezvous, male voyeurism, and forceful male entry when women bathed brought fines, exile, and even death. In the scene above, bathing women are completely naked in the presence of a male attendant (upper right), who discreetly wears bikini-like underpants, the string of which can be seen tied at his hip. According to legal, literary, and private records, men and women as a rule bathed in such discreet, if scanty, attire, the male underpants matched by the woman's "bath honor"—a thin shirt veiling her body from shoulders to thighs.

This bold portrayal of female nudity tells the other side of the story and of human nature. The artist magnifies the human form for a private patron who fancied complete nudity as well; outfitting the subjects with undergarments and shirts would have defeated the wishes of both. From Max Geisberg, *The German Single-Leaf Woodcut, 1500–1550,* vol. 1, ed. Walter L. Stauss (New York: Hacker Art Books, 1974), p. 244. By permission of Abaris Books. For interpretation, see Hans Peter Duerr, *Der Mythos vom Zivilisationsprozess,* vol. 1, *Nacktheit und Scham* (Frankfurt am Main, 1988), pp. 38–72, esp. 72.

The Thenn Children by the Master of the Portraits of the Thenn Children (1516)

An unidentified Salzburg portraitist gained such renown from his portraits of these two handsome boys and their sister that he became known in history through their name. The boy on the left holds a bird in his right hand and a sack of bird seed in his left. The touching and romanticized portrayals of the Thenn children, each finely clothed, are set against luminous snowcapped mountains. By the sixteenth century, such realistic portrayals of children at the hands of skilled artists were commonplace and had numerous precedents in the late Middle Ages. By permission of Das Städelsches Kunstinstitut, Frankfurt am Main.

John Frederick of Saxony (1503–1554) by Lucas Cranach (1506)

Royally attired four-year-old crown prince and future Saxon elector John Frederick (r. 1532–1547) rides his pony at Coburg Castle, a favorite hunting retreat of his father and uncle, to one or both of whom he may be waving as he rides by. The castle and town, with its protective wall, are seen in the background, while Saxon coats of arms swing from the branches of an overhanging tree. John Frederick was the last of three Saxon electors court painter Lucas Cranach (1472–1553) served, immortalizing their persons, hunts, and tournaments for over fifty years—in John Frederick's case doing so from childhood through adulthood, the two men dying within a year of each other. By permission of Evamaria Brockhoff and Verlag Friedrich Pustet, Regensburg.

A Prolific and Well-Spoken Housewife by Petrarca-Meister (late fifteenth century)

In a well-ordered nursery, a patrician mother nurses her last born, while a nanny draws thread. The two attend eight children, who appear to have been born close together. The scene catches the father as he stops by on his way to work. His wife expresses her needs and wishes for the day, going beyond what he can remember or cares to hear, his right hand telling her "enough already." The well-equipped room has a potty chair (upper left) and a walker, and the well-dressed children enjoy several diversions. On the floor lie marbles and a top, but wooden kitchen spoons are momentarily the favored toys. The boy at the cradle rides a stick horse and holds a "windmill" decorated with a bee, which spins in the air as he gallops about. A bond of affection between the father and the children is suggested by the clinging daughter, who may be about to receive the necklace he holds in his left hand. From *Newe Kunstliche/wohlgerissene unnd in Holtz geschnittene Figuren . . . von den Fürtrefflichen . . . Mahlern/Reissern/und Formschneidern* (Frankfurt am Main: Vincenz Steinmeyer, 1620). By permission of the Department of Printing and Graphic Arts, Houghton Library, Harvard College Library.

Coping with Early Child Death (1620)

A mother who has lost a child mourns amid scenes of typical early child death—drowning in wells (lower left), being slaughtered by soldiers in time of war (center left), and falling from windows (upper right). In addition to viral diseases such as smallpox and measles, simple injuries incurred while running and playing also ended children's lives. Fathers writing end-of-year reports in family chronicles noted with thanksgiving when a child had had no "catastrophic falls." Because surgical treatment of deep wounds or gashes was still primitive and medications against infection unreliable, injuries sustained at play could be life-threatening. The accompanying caption presents a bittersweet consolation for bereaved parents at the death of an infant or toddler:

> Among the living everywhere, the very young perish first,
> And departing life join the angelic host.
> As soon as a child dies
> It becomes a playmate of the angels.
> A child can have no better luck
> Than to die on the day of its birth.

From *Newe Kunstliche/wohlgerissene unnd in Holtz geschnittene Figuren . . . von den Fürtrefflichen . . . Mahlern/Reissern/und Formschneidern* (Frankfurt am Main: Vincenz Steinmeyer, 1620). By permission of the Department of Printing and Graphic Arts, Houghton Library, Harvard College Library.

The Feast of St. Nicholas by Jan Steen (1663–1667)

The most popular Dutch family celebration was the feast day of St. Nicholas. Although Calvinist theologians condemned the feast because of its revering of saints, many Reformed (Protestant) families celebrated it. Here, seven children have opened presents left in their shoes and stockings the night before by St. Nick. Their mother, an apparent widow (no father appears in the scene), and two grandparents are with them. The focus, at the center, is on a seemingly spoiled daughter, who clutches a haloed St. John the Baptist (this detail suggests a Catholic family). In the background before the hearth, the youngest child, in the arms of her brother, holds a gingerbread St. Nick. On the left, an older brother cries because his shoe holds a birch switch, a punishing gift; this, together with the reaction of his siblings, suggests he is the family bully. The sister standing behind him delights in his misfortune, as does a younger brother, who holds a prized golf club from St. Nick. In the back an apparently merciful grandmother beckons to the boy to come and look behind the curtain, where a real present apparently awaits him. By permission of the Rijksmuseum, Amsterdam. Mariet Westermann, *The Amusements of Jan Steen: Comic Painting in the Seventeenth Century* (Zwolle, 1998), pp. 155–156; H. Perry Chapman et al., *Jan Steen: Painter and Storyteller* (New Haven, 1996), pp. 197–198.

Women Hunting Men by the Housebook Master (ca. 1480)

This parody of the noble stag hunt portrays lusty young noblewomen hunting a lesser game: young men. It is spring and desire is queen. Ignoring class lines and employing means both fair and foul, the women pursue busy, unsuspecting men as if they were small game. At the far right, a woman is perched in a window opposite a nesting stork, who cries for its mate. Another beckons across a well to a stableboy, who is feeding ducks. A third marches forth with a bird trap in hand, as a mother attempts in vain to restrain her. At the upper left a young farmer, enticed by a bucket of water, hangs upside down in a nag trap, as another hides in fear across from him in the bushes. In the foreground, two couples embrace, one lasciviously. Although not an actual scene a contemporary rider would likely have come upon at a fifteenth-century castle, much of real life is depicted, real desires transhistorically expressed, and the gender fantasies of noble males and females suggested. From *The World of the Medieval Housebook*, by permission of Prestel Verlag.

❧ 5 ❧

PARENTAL ADVICE

Between July 1533 and February 1534 the city of Nürnberg saw more than 5,000 of its 25,000 inhabitants fall victim to one of the worst plagues in the city's history. Among those escaping death was the merchant family of Linhart Tucher, co-head of the Nürnberg-based Tucher trading company, with posts across Europe and in the Near East. As with other Franconian merchant families pursuing international trade (Albrecht Dürer's among them), a Moor's head sat prominently atop the Tucher coat of arms—an image of the martyred St. Maurice (d. 287), who was both the patron saint of Nürnberg cloth-makers and the perfect talisman for merchants networking in Italy and the eastern Mediterranean. The prominence of this black saint on merchant coats of arms also proclaimed the openness, principled as well as pragmatic, of late medieval burgher society.[1]

In late summer 1533 plague began to invade Nürnberg, but Linhart and his wife, Katherina, could not then flee the city due to the demands of the family business. So a maternal aunt took their seven children to a safe refuge with relatives in Nördlingen, fifty-five miles away. During the subsequent six-and-a-half month separation, the parents wrote daily to the children, Linhart's every letter recorded in a specially made "copybook" along with his correspondence with relatives and friends in loco parentis there—in all, over two hundred letters back and forth. Neither the imperatives of business nor the threat of death diminished the cohesion and loyalty of the family; and, far from interrupting or overshadowing it, the larger worlds of household and kin complemented it perfectly as well. In this most crisis-ridden of times, this early-sixteenth-century family remained as tightly knit as ever.[2]

In 1539, a few years after the Tuchers were reunited with their children in Nürnberg, Augsburg merchant Leo Ravensburg sent his fourteen-year-old son even farther away from home—to the French city of Lyons, a major Tucher trading post three hundred miles from Nürnberg, where young Christoph would begin an apprenticeship. Before the boy departed, the father composed a personal letter of counsel and instruction, which his son was to carry with him, to read and ponder frequently en route and after settling in with his new master. In the letter, the father carefully stated parental expectations with regard to both the boy's moral and religious conduct and his vocational training. These ranged from commonsensical safety precautions (keeping his feet dry, accommodating foreign customs, avoiding treacherous swimming holes and thuggish hangouts) to career advice and admonitions on health- and success-threatening addictions or temptations (alcohol, gambling, stealing, prostitutes, and immature marriage).[3]

The parental conduct revealed and the concerns and advice expressed in Linhart Tucher's copybook and Leo Ravensburg's letter were as typical in the early sixteenth century as they would be in the instructions of responsible parents in the early twenty-first. Contrary to what historians of the 1970s and 1980s would have us believe, these parent-child relationships were not rare exceptions in an otherwise parentally indifferent and tyrannous family world. The everyday lessons of parenting and child rearing have remained consistent through the centuries in West European and Anglo-American cultures from the seventeenth century onward. When the children and wards of parents and guardians stumbled on the developmental and vocational tracks laid for them in adolescence and youth, those parents and guardians shared the same pain and exasperation of parents and guardians in antiquity and the Middle Ages.

In November 1669 the seventeen-year-old son of English Presbyterian minister Henry Newcome (1627–1695) informed his father that he had walked out of a carefully arranged apprenticeship that promised the youth a secure livelihood. The news crushed his father, who wrote of it the day he received the news:

> This night I had a letter . . . which brought me the saddest news that ever I had in my life, namely of the miscarriage of Daniel. It is a great sorrow, bitter, reaches to the very heart.[4]

Five months later, still with a sad heart, yet determined to make the best of his son's abilities, the father sent him "beyond seas . . . by Tangier, the Madeiras, Barbados, and so to Jamaica," where, with a new, second chance, he hoped his son would make his way in the New World with a merchant trader.[5]

Over the centuries, many another parent faced the challenge of a child who, whether due to weakness, ineptitude, or perversity, stopped before a jumpable hurdle, or succumbed to some self-defeating temptation or folly. In such circumstances, some parents collapsed with their children, while others looked the other way and went on with their lives. A great many others, however, dug in for the duration, dragging their children kicking and screaming into adulthood and useful citizenship rather than abandon them to their own hapless devices.

That was the reaction in 1687 of Mary Woodforde, second wife of Anglican clergyman Samuel, when she received the news that her son John faced expulsion from college and with it the sure loss of his planned career. With others, the boy had written frivolous and apparently vulgar rhymes, and after being given a second chance on his solemn oath of honor never so to indulge himself again, he was soon caught red-handed again. The punishment was now a caning. However, John and several of his comrades refused to be whipped, and their defiance now threatened expulsion.

Gathering her religious faith and parental devotion, Mrs. Woodforde implored both God and her husband to persuade the boy, for the sake of his own moral character and future career at a time when there was no other recourse, to change his mind and receive his punishment. On March 6, 1687, she recorded the episode in her diary.

> This evening I had the cutting news that my second boy
> John was in rebellion at the College at Winton, where he
> and [some of] his companions . . . [having been] called to
> be whipped for [writing forbidden verses] refused to be

punished . . . [and] must now be expelled [if they do not submit]. God, I beseech thee of thy great mercy to subdue all their stubborn hearts, and to give them grace to repent and accept the punishment due for their fault, and not to let them run to ruin, for Christ's sake.[6]

Two days later, following the father's visit to the school, Mrs. Woodforde thankfully recorded the boy's apparent change of heart.

Yesterday my dear husband went to Winton about Jack, and I have received this afternoon a letter from him which gives me hope that he has humbled himself, for which I from the bottom of my heart give most humble thanks to Almighty God.[7]

This mother's willingness, even insistence, that her son accept a caning for breaking his word was a decision few parents then questioned. It was also one few had to make. Long before they found themselves in so dire a state, parents in the past had at their disposal a large repertoire of argument and appeal designed to steady shaky children and adolescents and keep them on the straight path to maturity and self-sufficiency. In 1792, Johann Krause (1747–1843), court chaplain in Eisenberg, Germany, wrote an instruction for his eleven-year-old son Karl, encouraging him to think only of how to make himself "a useful and contributing member of human society."[8] The boy, who would grow up to be a well-known philosopher, had recently left home for the first time to begin a course of study at a cloister school. Along with stock advice on personal hygiene and safety, stewardship of his possessions, and tightfisted money management, the senior Krause particularly urged his son to master the art of advantageous association and networking. "Accommodate your fellow students and be friendly to each, as you must, but become close friends with only the best of them," by whom he meant those youth whose example, counsel, and position might help Karl reach his life goals.[9]

It was similar concern over bad associations that moved another father, Leipzig merchant Friedrich Perthes (1742–1843), to deny his son, a twenty-year-old theology student at the University of Tübingen, permission to join a fraternity. This father feared his son would fall prey to the "sensually minded" youths he believed dominated such associations. And even if his son should successfully resist his fraternity brothers' efforts to corrupt him, he would be shunned or otherwise punished for spurning their way of life.

This father did not believe that fraternities were the direst threat to his son's character and career. More dangerous still were the religious fanatics within the university, overly earnest, self-righteous, moralizing youth. These antitypes of the free-spirited fraternity brothers were perversely idealistic and made a mockery of youth by robbing it of its joy.

It is a failing of many youths in our time, among them quite a few who are of good will, that they want to be masters without having first put in their years as apprentices and journeymen. These are young people who exhibit a singlemindedness, an exactitude, and an efficiency so thorough[10] as to suggest the peace and solemnity of old age. They punish their bodies and are strict in their morals, a new breed of Stoics, whose condition makes a monstrosity out of youth. Few of them will save their souls in this way; and their contempt for the world and the riches of human life fills them with an unfeeling egoism that becomes in its later stages a self-defeating feeling of futility. Depending on one's strength of character and will, the end result can be inhumanity and criminality.[11]

Among such youth prematurely grown old are some who, misconstruing their religious feelings, wish to gain mastery immediately, and so lay down their arms before they have done battle with the inner and the outer world [and thoroughly discovered themselves]. Believing their lives have peaked already in youth,[12] they cry out prematurely: "All is vain; let us humbly surrender ourselves to the Lord!" Among them, however, are to be found few of the elect appointed by God to proclaim His honor . . . On the contrary, a great many only postpone the battle with themselves and the world until they reach their later years, by which time that battle is far more difficult and dangerous. Still others among them are brutalized by the formulaic lives they lead,[13] and many succumb to the most shameful hypocrisy.[14]

Parents and those who stood in loco parentis in the past recognized the dangers posed to the young by their idealism, which also sprang from a carefully cultivated conscience. A symbiotic relationship existed between the power of false prophets and the gullibility of their disciples. The same inner resources that helped the young maintain their vital self-confidence also made them vulnerable to the charms and deceits of gurus and hucksters. In one of the most famous eighteenth-century German parental instructions to a child, Hamburg poet and literary journal editor Matthias Claudius (1740–1815), who wrote voluminously to his ten children, explained to his eldest son, then sixteen and departing home to begin a merchant's apprenticeship, the difference between fakers and wise men.

> Be happy to learn from others, and where there is talk of wisdom, human happiness, light, freedom, and virtue, listen intently. But do not take what you hear for truth on the spot,[15] for not all clouds carry water, and there are sundry kinds. There are those who think they have mastered something when they can talk on and on about it. [But] words are only words, and when they sail forth quickly and glibly, be on your guard. The horses that pull wagons with [real] goods take slower strides. Accept

nothing from pushers; where haranguing occurs on the street, move along. If someone wants to teach you wisdom, look him straight in his face, and if he still thinks he can do so, be he ever so learned and famous, walk away and ignore what he says.[16]

Quaker Mary Sewell (1797–1884), mother of Anna Sewell (1820–1878), the author of *Black Beauty* (1877), believed she had found the secret to instilling a proper conscience in young children without jeopardizing their self-confidence: immerse them first in the knowledge of God's love and forgiveness, and then allow them to discover the dark side of their lives on their own.

> The first thing to teach a little child is that he has a Father in heaven who loves him and wishes him to be as happy as he can be . . . Do not too early impress upon the mind of a little child that he is a sinner; let him discover this by his own experience. When he does wrong, let the natural consequences of his wrongdoing fall upon him. Do not shield him from the consequences of ignorance or disobedience; let them fall with their full weight, but let them [also] be the only penalties. Let him distinctly feel in himself the difference between obedience and disobedience [and in this way] cultivate a quick and tender conscience.[17]

Around the turn of the nineteenth century, poet Johann
Gottfried Seume (1763–1810), then royal tutor to the young
Count G. A. O. von Ingelström, also directed his royal ward to
the qualities that should lie deep within every well-reared child.
The occasion of the advice was the young count's sixteenth
birthday, when he was preparing to depart home for the first
time and begin a life of military service abroad.

> Soon you will . . . enter the great theatre of the world . . .
> Once there, do not be too bold, but also do not tremble,
> for both extremes will run you all the sooner into the arms
> of danger . . . Do not enter the world zealously thinking
> you must make your fortune there; for the wise man al-
> ready has his fortune [within] and is not threatened when
> he meets its very opposite. Everything under the moon is
> uncertain and inconstant, so never place your entire hap-
> piness in anything outside yourself . . . Subject every-
> thing to your own reasons, and as little as you would
> make the judgment of others your guide, also do not im-
> pose your own opinion on them. Let self-persuasion be
> the most sacred thing. In this way, you will keep your self-
> respect, for whoever loses this has suffered irreparable
> loss.[18]

Because a tender life and a fledging career could be quickly
made or broken by a youngster's behavior in service, apprenticeship, and school—where parental salvage operations be-

came more difficult—the lessons learned at home were vital, and those teaching them knew they were involved in a fateful struggle. The dysfunctional family was no more a stranger to the past than it is today, but neither were clever and determined efforts to fix it. German philosopher Johann Georg Hamann (1730–1788) headed such a family, one torn apart by bitter conflict between himself and his son. Among his four children by a common-law wife was an only son, Johann Michael, with whom this father fought for years. At nineteen, the boy was sent away from the parental home in Königsberg to live with another family, where he might continue his schooling in a more peaceful environment.

On the day after his departure, the senior Hamann discovered a number of his own books and papers trashed and scattered about in his son's room, among them a coveted unbound volume of Shakespeare, which was covered with dust and filth. An undrunk glass of beer remained under the youth's bed—a departing gesture of disrespect, as nocturnal drinking had repeatedly been forbidden him. According to the father, the emptiness the boy attempted unsuccessfully to fill by drinking was actually an unquenchable "desire for the forbidden." That became the subject of his first letter to the son at his new residence.

I know how much the bewitching sin of disobedience reigns in my house, and how little influence the promises of the fourth commandment ["Honor your father and mother that your days may be long"] have on your sentiments and behavior, despite my pleas. However, between the two evils, I prefer your disobedience to deceitful and slavish lip-service. Still, if you do not fear God, what can it matter if you despise and mock me as well? If you do not love God, I have no desire to be your idol [in His place]. Johann Michael, if you can so soon forget your baptismal covenant[19] and the promises verified by your recent confirmation, then you may as well forget everything I have taught you and expect no new instructions from me. "You are already filled, you are already rich, you reign without us" (1 Cor. 4:8). If you feel no duty to the fourth commandment, I will become as dumb [to you] as you are deaf [to me] . . . I deeply wish that you might believe how much the blessing, or the curse, of that commandment affects one's entire life—how our hearts need to be prepared and inclined by it to a true love of our neighbor—and not have to learn this lesson by [bitter] experience . . .

What an abomination of desolation proceeds from the mischievous whims that move you to steal, and from the invincible stubbornness that resists all discipline and deliberation . . . Instead of inciting you to your duties, my reminders only make you more indifferent and give you further reason to defy. In my burning desire to serve your best interests, you suspect only ill-humor on my part. That is why I lose all courage and hope of ever having a happy relationship with you . . .[20]

Ask yourself what has moved you to trash my papers, to drag into your room all the things of mine that I found on the floor, to throw them all over the place and leave them lying about, disposing of my things as if you were their lord, and ruining so many of my books and papers without knowing why or to what end—and all the while ignoring my every request, exhortation, and warning.

If you do not renounce Appolyon and Abaddon,[21] the spirit of indiscipline and desolation, and God does not give you a new heart to go with your new home, then I have wished your removal from my house in vain . . .[22]

Philosopher Hamann was not alone in finding himself incapable of washing his hands of a defiant or ne'er-do-well child. Forbearance and a fresh (if lesser) opportunity to succeed were rather the rule, parents in the past being as loath to see a child fail completely as their most devoted modern counterparts. However, those same parents believed even more deeply in the redemptive power of "tough love," particularly when the point of no return between parent and child had clearly been reached.

The famous Göttingen mathematician, astronomer, and physicist Carl Friedrich Gauss (1777–1855) is a case in point. He struggled for years with his son Eugen (b. 1811), who was a failure at the university and at everything else he tried. At twenty-one, he migrated to America, arriving broke and unable to find work. Moved by necessity, he enlisted in the military—in the past, often the vocation of last resort for a failed well-to-do son[23]—only to discover that he was also not cut out for a soldier's life. Turning again to his father for a quick rescue, he begged the senior Gauss's support in helping him muster out immediately. His father instead pointed out the advantages of his present circumstances and suggested that he might try to view them as a last, best chance to learn personal responsibility.

> I can only view your repeated demand to be free from the profession of arms as groundless, wrong-headed, and contrary to your own best interests, hence one I dare not grant . . . After giving it thought, you too must readily agree that suddenly to be free from your present circumstances would only toss you back up in the air. You yourself have blocked your return to Europe, since your entire life to this point has become only too well known here. [And as much as I know about that life] so little do I know what you should now undertake in America. [What is clear is that] the time has come for your desultory dawdling to end once and for all.

On the positive side, your subsistence for the time being is assured you in your present situation [in the military], which is also an inducement for you to begin to prepare for a sensible future life. And the region in which your company is stationed provides you many opportunities to get to know the [German] immigrants who have settled there, also to study the land and its customs. By good behavior and active devotion to duty, it should not be difficult for you, nor take you long, to advance at least to the rank of corporal. Then, you may earn the favor and good will of your superiors, and when you are honorably discharged, their counsel and contacts may significantly aid and abet your further progress [in a civilian career] . . .

Meanwhile, womanish wailing over the difficulty of a situation you alone, heedless of all restraint, created for yourself will find only a deaf ear with your father. However, evidence that you are confronting your situation sensibly—recognizing [the military] to be a school for self-improvement and honestly making the most of it in preparation for a new life in the New World—that will find an open ear with your father. I am talking about a life in which industry, moderation, prudence, discipline, and honesty become second nature to you and you find it within your power, for the first time, to be a useful and successful citizen of the world.[24]

The senior Gauss punctuated his warning with news of the recent death of Eugen's mother and, contrary to what the boy might reasonably have expected, the availability to him of a maternal inheritance of 4,500 taler. The inheritance would, however, be awarded only under the following conditions. After the passage of six years (that is, in 1838), upon proof of self-improvement, he might collect the accumulated interest, and assuming he was still gainfully employed after five more years, the capital would become his as well.[25]

Armoring Daughters

As with the rearing of sons, no parental action was thought to contribute more to the fitness and success of a daughter than the laying of a sound moral and spiritual foundation early in life. Such a foundation was believed to be even more important for daughters than for sons. Males might have in addition to their piety and charm both greater education and worldly experience on which to draw in the face of moral hazard, whereas young females had to rely almost entirely on piety, demeanor, and wit to escape the temptations that threatened their character and reputation. Still, the double standard by which male and female behavior was judged until recent times permitted society, incongruously, to be more forgiving of the failures of sexually promiscuous and adulterous men.

In the preparation of his six daughters for passage into adulthood, sixteenth century Count Palatine Johann II (1584–1635) alternated small carrots with large sticks. Early in her life, second daughter Elisabeth (b. 1613) was sent to the castle of her grandmother to be raised. Over the years, her father remained a forceful presence in her life via the mail, reminding her of the things she should keep foremost in mind. He also sent her modest gifts while promising bigger ones if the progress reports on her conduct and studies remained good. At the same time, he made clear the consequences of a bad report. Along with an article of clothing, the girl received the following instruction from her father when she was eight.

> Because I see that you have learned to write so neatly, I am sending you a remembrance, and should you continue to make such progress and to be very devout, I will send you something even prettier. Be especially respectful of [your] esteemed grandmother, who showers so many kindnesses on you, and always obey her will. Otherwise, I will never be fond of you. I am happy to hear that you are well, but not as happy as when I hear that you are being good, studying diligently, and doing what one tells you.[26]

Two years later, the count's advice and tactics had not changed.

> So that you may know that I am thinking of you, I am sending with this letter some fine satin for a skirt, which your esteemed grandmother will give you if you are good. And if you will continue to be obedient and sub-

missive to Her Grace, I will remain fond of you and send you more.[27]

Two years later, Elisabeth, now twelve, still received small gifts wrapped in large warnings.

> Nothing you do could give me more joy than to know that you are continuing to earn your grandmother's care and attention . . . by childlike obedience and devotion to duty, also that you are treating her and all the other esteemed relatives there . . . with respect. Above all else, keep your eyes always on God so that he will stand by you [and] behave in such a way that one there has reason to continue to treat you kindly. Then you will also give me reason to love you and to treat you as a true father should. Be godfearing and humble toward everyone, and I will always remain your dear, loyal father.[28]

Two centuries later, Prince Carl of Hohenzollern (1785–1853), a father who gave carrots far more comfortably than he shook sticks, presented his fourteen-year-old daughter Caroline with a similar prescription for well-being and success. At age twelve, the girl left for Paris and private tutoring, and the following year her brother also began a course of study abroad. That the father missed them both is made clear by his letter, which explained to Caroline why children must be sent away from home at young ages.

The end of this year (1823) is marked again by a painful separation. Last year, my dear Caroline left the parental home. Now it is dear Carl who left us toward the end of the month . . . Without the recognition that this separation is required for the well-being of beloved children, these partings would remain very saddening. However, it is the duty of parents to make this sacrifice, and at the same time the obligation of [absent] children to apply themselves fully [in their new environments], using this time well to improve themselves in heart and soul. In this way, they can repair the tender feelings of their parents [who miss them]![29]

Unlike the young countess Elisabeth, princess Caroline was not, however, a capable student. So poorly written did her father find her letters ("bad handwriting, misspellings, constant repetition, evidence of disinterest, little attention to style") that he kept them away from her siblings to spare the family embarrassment. Seizing upon the occasion of the girl's approaching birthday, he reiterated a proven formula for self-improvement.

You are now almost fifteen, and given what you have learned so far, I hope you can comprehend the high obligation and benefits of completing what you have started. You seem to me not to have progressed as far in your education as a girl of your age is normally expected to do! If you [too] are convinced of this, then hold fast to your religious feelings, which I recognized early in you and still observe with peace of mind. If your feelings for your loving parents, grandparents, and siblings . . . remain [as I remember them], then it will be evident to you that you must now devote all your energies and will to your education and show yourself to be both pleasing to God and grateful to your parents.

Time is precious, so ponder well that opportunities now squandered cannot later be recovered. All the sacrifices that are now being made on your behalf by your caring father, who loves you very much, are lost if there is no sincere will and determination on your side to gain good and useful knowledge and acquire agreeable skills! Success is unthinkable without effort! If you devote yourself to your work with sure purpose and firm resolve, this year will surely be the one that decides your future!

Dear Caroline, do consider your father's wishes, so that when we meet, I may . . . find my love and concern for you repaid and your birthday promise ["to do everything" to make me happy] confirmed![30]

The virtues that made possible a daughter's success in service and school also put her in a stronger position to resist the temptations of the opposite sex, which parents knew could undermine a daughter's future as surely as any dread disease or misstep on the vocational ladder. Not all parents were prepared to restrict their children in this regard as severely as a seventeenth-century mother from Quitzau, who left behind the following advice to her two daughters:

> [At] parties . . . accept drinks only from other girls. If a boy peels a fruit for you, do not accept it. When boys come and sit beside you, don't answer their questions; say only "yes," "no," and "I don't know"; and do not smile at them. When boys happen to come into your bedroom, hide behind the bed and hit them in the face.[31]

The ability to negotiate a man's world without coming to harm has always been a daughterly skill highly prized by parents. That thoughtful parents pondered and communicated it well is suggested by the instruction of a late-eighteenth-century Edinburgh physician on the conduct becoming a woman who finds herself in the company of men.

> Converse with men, even of the first rank, with that dignified modesty which may prevent the approach of the most distant familiarity and consequently prevent them from feeling themselves to be your superiors. Wit is the most dangerous talent you can possess. It must be guarded with great discretion and good nature, otherwise it will create you many enemies. [For while it] is perfectly consistent with softness and delicacy . . . it is so flattering to vanity that those who possess it [can] become intoxicated with it and lose all self-command. Humour is a different quality. It will make your company much solicited,

but . . . it is often a great enemy to delicacy, and a still greater one to dignity of character. It may sometimes gain you applause, but it will never procure you respect. [Also] be ever cautious in displaying your good sense, or it will be thought that you assume a superiority over the rest of your company. And if you happen to have any learning, keep it a profound secret, especially from the men who generally look with a jealous and malignant eye on a woman of great parts and a cultivated understanding.[32]

Parents also worried about the despoliation of their sons by loose or conniving women. When seventeen-year-old Karl Theodor Körner, son of Dresden civil servant Christian Körner (1756–1831), entered the mining school in Freiberg to prepare for university study in the natural sciences, his father sent him, among other pieces of advice, the following reflections on the rewards of sexual abstinence and purity.

I hear much about the corruption of morals in Freiberg and of the enticements of immoral prostitutes there. However, I am not now worried about you. You have an aversion to depravity that will not permit you to be led astray by libertines eager to teach you their ways. I have observed with delight your esteem for the female gender and your receptiveness to its charms. Such respect is good protection against the excesses of raw sensuality. Happy is the man who can one day stand before his beloved [bride] with a pure soul and an unimpaired body! You know the popular poem, "He who never in the lap of lust [has lain] . . ." Schönberger[33] and Father have never regretted that they refused to reduce themselves to animals, saving the highest sensual pleasure for the moment when it could be ennobled by the inner union of [their] souls. Such things should not be discussed with profane people. But there are also estimable people who, to their misfortune, behave like animals when it comes to sex.[34] To wish to change them is wasted effort; however, one also does not have to allow them to be one's guide—and ways can always be found to elude their suggestions in particular instances without having to share one's innermost feelings.[35]

Infrastructure

If parental advice to the young in centuries past might be marshaled into one sentence, it would be the priority of self-knowledge and self-mastery: think first not what should be made of the world, but what must be done with oneself. As famed English statesman and author Lord Chesterfield (1694–1773) put it to his own son in the mid-eighteenth century:

In order to judge of the inside of others, study your own, for [people] in general are very much alike. Though one has one prevailing passion and another another, their operations are much the same; whatever engages or disgusts, pleases or offends you in others, will, *mutatis mutandis,* engage, disgust, please, or offend others in you. So observe with the utmost attention all the operations of your own mind, the nature of your own passions, and the various motives that determine your will, and you may come to know in a great degree all mankind.[36]

As harsh as the advice of the past may at times appear to be to a modern reader, those who gave it did so in the belief that they were passing on the wisdom of the ages and guarding civilization's gates. Even in the early twentieth century, German poet Richard Dehmel (1863–1920) could write with similar assurance to his nineteen-year-old son, who had asked his father's permission to withdraw from a promising apprenticeship, apparently in manufacturing or engineering, after having devoted considerable time and effort to it. The youth had suddenly found such practical training tedious and now was of the opinion that an artisan's or craftman's life was beneath his intellectual talents, which he now hoped to develop in a liberal arts course of study at the university. In a blunt letter, reassuringly signed "your nondictatorial father," the senior Dehmel opposed the requested transfer as precipitous, arrogant, and wrong-headed. But he worried most that such a change might put at risk something more important to his son's happiness and success than the choice of a career, namely, his self-respect, should he so lightly remove his hand from the plough.

ANCESTORS

I will tell you something, my boy, not as a father, but as an older friend, who in his own green youth had plagued himself with exactly the same scruples you now are having. Today, I am very grateful to my father, who at the time simply commanded: "Do your duty, or go to the dogs!" There is only one way to gain self-respect, and that is to finish each task one has begun, whether one likes it or not. Also, there is no physical labor that could not also be called intellectual as well. Do you believe that [architect] Cockerell and [merchant] Cobden,[37] or any other artisans with a world-wide reputation, are not also "intellectual" workers? If you believe you can resolve your inner conflict by "art and science," just ponder again the meaning of the timeless story of Prometheus's vulture! No intellectual work is brought to completion without constant self-laceration; the price of every happiness is much pain, and the greatest happiness of all is called victory over self, or, at least, self-control.

I give you my sincere advice: before leaving [your apprenticeship], at least take the journeyman's exam—as a test of your energy, as it were! You can then always study [at the university]. And if that study does not satisfy you, you will have still laid a surer foundation for yourself, on which you can again set your feet . . .[38]

Such sentiments, extending into the twentieth century, reverberate from antiquity through ages now lost, their original societies and cultures forever beyond our reach. Yet the continuity of human experience within both the more primitive and the exalted world of family and household remains palpable and compelling. Who does not find courtship and marriage, childbearing and child rearing, and the succession of new generations—wherever and whenever they occur—familiar in any age? The most consistent and worthy lessons of history, both the do's and the don'ts, appear to have crystallized in the annals of the family.

✲ 6 ✲

FAMILY ARCHIVES

From ancient Roman marriage practices, to seventeenth-century funeral sermons,[1] to advice literature extending into the twentieth century, historians find abundant features of the "modern sentimental family" existing from antiquity through the Renaissance. German historian Erich Maschke, writing in 1980, chose the phrase "accentuated with feeling"[2] to dismiss Edward Shorter's depiction of the premodern family's alleged emotional and moral vacuity and his celebratory portrayal of its 1960s counterpart. In making his case, Maschke drew on account books (economic records sometimes containing surprising personal information), diaries, wills, and family chronicles surviving from the late fourteenth and fifteenth centuries.

Thanks to the availability of cheap, durable paper and inks and the assistance of newly invented vernacular writing guides, the urban laity were also beginning to add collections of valued letters to their family archives. Both immediate and detailed, this "pragmatic epistolography"[3] has made it possible for modern readers to share the authors' daily activities and innermost thoughts. In such materials, historians and genealogists find first-person accounts of that "self-fashioning" for which twentieth-century historians have hunted—only here with neither the coercive atmosphere of visitational and inquisitional records, nor the need for the intellectual contortions often forced upon historians when the sources they consult are completely impersonal and oblique. A picture or an icon may be worth a thousand words, and it may be deconstructed into as many more, but a family archive *is* a thousand words and more.

A daily diary entry or a personal letter may be as contrived as any end-of-life autobiography, but in their essence they are occasional and spontaneous means of communication, earnest messages frequently executed on the run, and with a specific event and/or person in mind. Particularly in correspondence between family members, colleagues, friends, and lovers, where clarity and truth have a premium and can be matters of life or death, "live" personal reactions to people, experiences, and events have been preserved as reliably as can be done in histori-

cal sources. Full of factual information—news of breaking
events or the comings and goings of relatives and acquain-
tances, instructions for some pressing chore or duty—the
unique feature of such letters is the frank sharing of private
life.[4] Nineteenth-century historian Georg Steinhausen, who pi-
oneered the study of medieval letters, believed that vernacular
correspondence cut across social boundaries and conveyed in
plain words the "emotional signature of an age,"[5] and did so no
less accurately than political and economic records preserved
and revealed an age's material life.

Between 1400 and 1800, surviving letters and other first-
person accounts come almost entirely from those with a degree
of literacy, mostly city-dwellers. Dictation, however, allowed
some actual or functional illiterates, for example, saints and
criminals, to leave behind lasting personal records as well.
What these sources lack in representativeness they more than
make up for in depth and opportunity for precise analysis. Such
sources give entry to the private worlds of their subjects at an
emotional and intellectual level rarely accessible through any
other contemporary record. Here the people of the past convey
both the story of their lives and what they personally made of
them.

To belittle or dismiss such sources on the grounds that they
do not represent society as a whole (no document can) is like

saying that one must drink the whole ocean before one may be certain it is salty. To surrender this most direct and intimate access to the past, and thereby to be forced to rely on secondary and tertiary reports of inquisitors, visitors, and postevent chroniclers for our best knowledge, would be a great defeat for both a present that wants to know and a past that wishes to be remembered. Still more tempting, but perilous, would be to find ourselves left to the supposedly transhistorical models of modern social science for our best knowledge of the past—as if the past were not a different time and place and capable of reliable study through its own hard sources and clear words.

The dismissal of first-person sources on the basis of their singularity presumes that other, superior contemporary sources exist for a deep study of the past from which accurate generalizations can be made. But here the key question must be: generalizations about what? What do we want to know about the past that is both true to it and useful to us? If the goal is to count in the remains of a church register the baptisms, marriages, and deaths in a parish; or to estimate from a surviving census the number of inmates in the households of a village or a town; or to determine from guild records how many women apprenticed in one or another trade over a period of time—then a degree of reliable descriptive information can indeed be placed in our hands. But what can we learn about the subjects themselves beyond their numbers and about ourselves in the long perspective of time? As a rule, the more numerically representative a source, the more limited, impersonal, and uninterpreted the qualitative information it conveys and in turn the more speculative the conclusions drawn.

By contrast, the study of family archives in historical context offers both a mass of quantitative data about and qualitative interpretation by the very subjects themselves. If, in such single cases, one cannot generalize across entire groups and societies, one may still critically hold a particular case or cases up to reigning generalizations derived from broader, but shallower, sources and articulated by numerous, but oblique and often uninvolved, commentators. Because mature family archives contain the fullest first-person accounts of the past—and as a rule document their subjects' interaction with the larger social, political, and cultural worlds they inhabit—those archives, wherever they exist, should be the historian's first point of entry into an age.[6] Otherwise, we may find ourselves at the very outset, when it makes all the difference, denying contemporaries the opportunity to speak as clearly, freely, and fully of their times as they might.

When asked why he robbed banks, notorious American thief Willie Sutton answered famously "Because that's were the money is." A hard-pressed family historian, asked why he or she studies family archives, might answer similarly: "Because that's where the richest information is." Banks, of course, are not the only places where money is to be found, nor are family archives the only sources of deep information about our ancestors. However, in both cases they remain, respectively and comparatively, the places where a great deal of money and information has accumulated in the most reliable and orderly form. And despite the hurdles that still remain in accessing them, the rewards in both cases can be very great.

In regard to the topics addressed in this book, family archives compellingly document the folly and hubris of assigning quintessential spousal and parental love only to modern or recent times. Such high qualities prove to be specific to family life itself and not to time and place—this notwithstanding the very different public faces that time and place always affix to particular ages and cultures. From this point of view, the evidence suggests that the "modern sentimental family" exists as far back in time and as widely in space as there are proper sources to document it.

Microhistorical studies of family archives and pioneering work on gender have broken new ground for the study of families in the past. In doing so they have exposed the strengths and the weaknesses of the Arièsian myth of a steadily evolving sentimental family over the last five centuries. With the resolution of Ariès's famous question of whether or not parents in the past recognized and treated their children as such (they emphatically did), historians may explore the primary sources of family history on more pertinent issues.

One is the reception of the changing imperatives of state, church, and popular culture within a highly self-conscious and comparatively fixed familial world, where men, women, and children recognize a history of their own in, with, around, and under the larger political, social, and cultural history of their times. Nowhere in the premodern world do court, city, and countryside—the lives of royals, burghers, and simple folk, the upper, middle, and lower classes—interact more often and revealingly than in urban family circles, where the comings and goings of each are preserved in the private records they kept. In those records—beyond literature and art, theology and law, and all the alleged transhistorical models of individual and social behavior—one may discover just how influential church, state, and popular culture were in the lives of people in the past.

Family archives also promise to shed new light on other unresolved problems: when the "modern" self appeared; whether women had a Renaissance and a Reformation; the degree to which smaller social entities, such as the family, were merely "farm teams" for the values of larger ones, such as the church or state; and what it meant in the past to be a man or a father, a woman or a mother, a child, teenager, and young adult. All of this information comes by way of comparatively reliable contemporary voices not easily ventriloquized by modern authorities.

Because history is the only deep, empirical record of human behavior we have, it is imperative that new generations on the brink of an unknown future possess the fairest and most accurate information about preceding ones. If in meeting that future the inertia of the past is an enemy, knowledge of the past is a proven friend of enlightened transition and reform. Rare are leaders and reformers who succeed for long by ignoring, twisting, or suppressing the proven lessons of the past. The most successful understood their place in time and invoked the past against both its worst self and the contemporary world they would change, confronting phonies and travesties with the battle cries of a stronger "tradition" and the cumulative truth of lived experience—from bibles, charters, and consitutions, to pivotal declarations and orations, to empirical facts and common sense.

For a modern age faced with a family crisis, there is good news from the recovered history of the family: this smallest and seemingly most fragile of institutions is proving itself to be humankind's bedrock as well as its fault line. Its strength lies in the cohesion and loyalty of the parent-child unit around which the larger worlds of household and kin, community and nation, and the global village necessarily revolve. Among these various social worlds, only the family creates itself virtually from nothing and gives life and stability to the others. The family is the great survivor amid the changing ages and cultures that envelop, shape, and test it for a while, only to run their course and pass away. Far from obstructing the modern family's future, the family of the past is an eternal spring from which present generations may draw their truest knowledge of self and the courage to soldier on.

NOTES

INTRODUCTION

1. Pierre Manent, *The City of Man,* trans. Mark A. LePain (Princeton, 1998), ch. 1.

2. Anticipations of the modern family are recognized in earlier centuries where parental occupations made possible a separation of home and workplace, as in the case of outworkers in rural industries, civil servants, and the Protestant clergy. Where family life developed within a sphere separate and distinct from the workaday world, "a favorable setting for the emergence of the new model burgher family" is said to exist. Richard van Dülmen, *Kultur und Alltag in der Frühen Neuzeit,* vol. 1 (Munich, 1990), pp. 19–20. Dülmen distinguishes six types of early modern households, two of which fall into this category. Ibid., pp. 15–18, 44–47. On kinder and gentler patriarchs in these early centuries, see Scott Hendrix, "Masculinity and Patriarchy in the Reformation," *Journal of the History of Ideas* 56 (1995):

177–193. Ulinka Rublack finds fathers directly assisting in childbirth, male prisoners released from prison when their wives approach full term. "Pregnancy, Childbirth, and the Female Body in Early Modern Germany," *Past and Present* 150 (1996): 84–110; cf. Ozment, "The Family in Reformation Germany: The Bearing and Rearing of Children," *Journal of Family History* 8 (1983): 159–176.

I. STRUCTURE AND SENTIMENT

1. Michael Anderson, *Approaches to the History of the Western Family* (Cambridge, 1994), p. 51. One can also cite subterreanean factors such as inflation, subliminal assumptions such as racism and sexism, and assumed conditions such as high mortality, all of which obliquely affect attitude and behavior.

2. Ibid., pp. 4–24. See also John Hajnal, "European Marriage Patterns in Perspective," in D. V. Glass and D. E. C. Eversley, eds., *Population in History* (Chicago, 1965), pp. 101–143, and Peter Laslett, "Characteristics of the Western Family Considered over Time," *Journal of Family History* 1 (1972): 89–115.

3. "It is one thing to propose plausible structurally-based transformations and quite another to document their precise impact on family attitudes and behavior and to rule out cultural interpretations . . . " Anderson, *Approaches*, p. 66. By so juxtaposing structural and cultural interpretations, Anderson may himself may be overlooking the ability of cultural interpretations to become self-confident universals. See Claudia Opitz, "Neue Wege der Sozialgeschichte? Ein kritischer Blick auf Otto Brunners Konzept des 'ganzen Hauses,'" *Geschichte und Gesellschaft* 20 (1994): 88–98.

4. James Casey, *The History of the Family* (Oxford, 1989), ch. 1, esp. p. 14.

5. Heide Wunder, *"Er ist die Sonn', sie ist der Mond": Frauen in der Frühen Neuzeit* (Munich, 1992), pp. 94–95; English: *He Is the Sun, She Is the Moon: Women in Early Modern Germany,* trans. Thomas Dunlap (Cambridge, Mass., 1998). See the vast and now even redundant literature on the difficulties of both patriarchs *(Hausväter)* and rulers *(Landesväter)* in "ordering" the lives of their households and subjects in early modern German lands: Thomas Max Safley, *Let No Man Put Asunder: The Control of Marriage in the German Southwest, 1550–1600* (Kirksville, Mo., 1984); Thomas Robisheaux, *Rural Society and the Search for Order in Early Modern Germany* (Cambridge, 1989); Gerald Strauss, *Luther's House of Learning: Indoctrination of the Young in the German Reformation* (Baltimore, 1978) and *Law, Resistance, and the State: The Opposition to Roman Law in Reformation Germany* (Princeton, 1986); Joel F. Harrington, *Reordering Marriage and Society in Reformation Germany* (Cambridge, 1995), esp. pp. 273–278; Heinz Schilling, *Religion, Political Culture and the Emergence of Early Modern Society: Essays in German and Dutch History* (Leiden, 1992); and Mack Walker, *German Home Towns. Community, State, and General Estates, 1648–1871* (Ithaca, 1971).

6. Casey, *History of the Family,* ch. 2; David Herlihy, *Medieval Households* (Cambridge, Mass., 1985), pp. 112–156; Donald Weinstein and R. N. Bell, *Saints and Society: The Two Worlds of Western Christendom, 1000–1700* (Chicago, 1982). On the rarity of penetrating sources such as the twelfth-century letters of Abelard and Heloise and the problem such scarcity poses, see M. T. Clanchy, *Abelard: A Medieval Life* (Oxford, 1997), pp. 11–19. For a discussion of the fullest quantitative record of family structure and organi-

zation in a Renaissance city, see the classic study of the Florentine catasto by David Herlihy and Christiane Klapisch-Zuber, *Tuscans and Their Families: A Study of the Florentine Catasto of 1427* (New Haven, 1985).

7. Mathias Beer, *Eltern und Kinder des späten Mittelalters in ihren Briefen: Familienleben in der Stadt des Spätmittelalters und der frühen Neuzeit mit besonderer Berücksichtigung Nürnbergs (1400–1550)* (Nürnberg, 1990), pp. 31–71; Rudolf Hirsch, *Printing, Selling, and Reading, 1450–1550* (Wiesbaden, 1967).

8. *L'Enfant et la vie familiale sous l'ancien regime* (Paris, 1960). The English translation appeared in 1962 under the title *Centuries of Childhood: A Social History of Family Life*, trans. Robert Baldick (New York, 1962). On the reception of Ariès, see Mathias Beer, "Kinder in den Familien deutscher Städte des späten Mittelalters und der frühen Neuzeit," *Zeitschrift für Kulturwissenschaften* 6 (1994): 25–48; Pia Haudrup Christensen, "Children as the Cultural Other: The Discovery of Children in the Social Cultural Sciences," in ibid., 1–16; Lawrence Stone, "The Massacre of the Innocents," *New York Review of Books* (November 14, 1974): 25–31; and Klaus Arnold, *Kind und Gesellschaft im Mittelalter und Renaissance* (Paderborn, 1980), pp. 11–15.

9. *Centuries of Childhood*, pp. 369–370.

10. "The discovery of childhood began in the thirteenth century, and its progress can be traced in the history of art in the fifteenth and sixteenth centuries. But the evidence of its development became more plentiful and significant from the end of the 16th and throughout the seventeenth." Ibid., p. 47.

11. Ibid., chs. 3–5.

12. "People could not allow themselves to become too attached to something that was regarded as a possible loss." Ibid., p. 39. The alleged effects of high infant mortality is a popular theme of the so-called "sentiment's school" of family history. Anderson, *Approaches*, ch. 3. Lawrence Stone perceived parental "limitation of psychological involvement with infant children" in the recycling of names of deceased siblings, a practice said to indicate "a lack of sense that the child was a unique being." Lawrence Stone, *The Family, Sex, and Marriage in England 1500–1800*, abbr. ed. (New York, 1977), pp. 55, 57. An alternative explanation of "same-naming" (a family's determination to continue a prominent or favored family name) is persuasively offered by Beer, *Eltern und Kinder*, pp. 232–234. See examples in Steven Ozment, *Flesh and Spirit: A Study of Private Life in Early Modern Germany* (New York, 1999), chs. 2, 5.

13. Ariès, *Centuries of Childhood*, pp. 128; 375ff.

14. Ibid., p. 128.

15. Ibid., pp. 375, 390, 403.

16. Compare the very similar description of the social bonds of traditional Catholic society in the Middle Ages, drawn polemically against the Reformation, in John Bossy, *Christendom and the West, 1400–1700* (New York, 1985), and Eamon Duffy, *The Stripping of the Altars* (New Haven, 1995).

17. "One is tempted to conclude that sociability and the concept of the family were incompatible and could develop only at each other's expense." Ariès, *Centuries of Childhood*, p. 407.

18. Ibid., pp. 413, 415.

19. See the examples of apprentice Michael Behaim and student Friedrich Behaim, in Steven Ozment, *Three Behaim Boys: Growing Up in Early Modern Germany* (New Haven, 1990), pp. 11–92, 93–159; Ilana Krausman Ben-Amos, *Adolescence and Youth in Early Modern England* (New Haven, 1994), pp. 102–103, 158–165, 173–175; and Barbara Hanawalt, *Growing Up in Medieval London* (Oxford, 1993), chs. 8, 10.

20. *Centuries of Childhood*, pp. 372–373. On Salic and other medieval law codes, see Gerhard Köbler, "Das Familienrecht in der spätmittelalterlichen Stadt," in Alfred Haverkamp, ed., *Haus und Familien in der spätmittelalterlichen Stadt* (Köln, 1984), p. 141; Peter Ketch, *Frauen im Mittelalter, 2: Frauenbild und Frauenrechte in Kirche und Gesellschaft. Quellen und Materialien*, ed. Annette Kuhn (Düsseldorf, 1984), pp. 180–181; Paula S. Fichtner, *Primogeniture and Protestantism in Early Modern Germany* (New Haven, 1989); and (in dialogue with Fichtner) Judith J. Hurwich, "Inheritance Practices in Early Modern Germany," *Journal of Interdisciplinary History* 23 (1993): 699–718. On children as successful *accusing* agents in witch trials (that is, identifying their parents as witches), see below, ch. 4, n. 1.

21. *The European Family: Patriarchy to Partnership from the Middle Ages to the Present*, trans. Karla Oosterven and Manfred Hörzinger (Chicago, 1983; original German, 1970). See my review in *Journal of the History of the Behavioral Sciences* 9 (1986). The effusive praise comes from Peter Laslett, then director of the Cambridge Research Group on Population Studies, in the foreword to the English translation, p. vii.

22. Mitterauer and Sieder, *European Family*, p. 7. In making their argument, the authors target the work of French historian Frédéric LePlay (d. 1882), *La Réforme sociale en France*, vol. 2 (Paris, 1864),

which favorably compared the preindustrial family with an allegedly unstable, impersonal, egoistic, hedonistic modern industrial counterpart. Mitterauer and Sieder, *European Family,* pp. 25–26, 37–41. On this issue, see Casey, *History of the Family,* pp. 11–14, and Anderson, *Approaches,* pp. 9–16.

23. Mitterauer and Sieder, *The European Family,* pp. 100, 127–128. Dülmen also maintains that the quality of marital sex between upper- and middle-class partners was better in the eighteenth century than in earlier times, thanks to a new "sensitizing of feelings." *Kultur und Alltag,* p. 191. On the ability of people in distant centuries to enjoy healthy sex lives, see James A. Brundage, *Law, Sex, and Christian Society in Medieval Europe* (Chicago, 1987); Harrington, *Reordering Marriage and Society,* passim (under fornication); and Ozment, *Flesh and Spirit,* ch. 1.

24. On the loss or diminishment of the family's traditional religious, judicial, protective, economic, reproductive, cultural, and educational functions after the Industrial Revolution, see Mitterauer and Sieder, *European Family,* ch. 4.

25. Ibid., pp. 60–63, 86–88, 104, 109–112, 128. The authors describe their scholarship on the family as morally superior to older "totalitarian" and "fascist" treatments "hostile to democracy and the emancipation of women." Ibid., pp. 2, 21, 25–26, 44, 86–87, 109, 117.

26. Edward Shorter, *The Making of the Modern Family* (New York, 1975), p. 227.

27. Ibid., pp. 61, 76. Compare Gene Brucker's gloomy conclusions about Italian marriage, drawn from court records (*Giovanni and Lusanna: Love and Marriage in Renaissance Florence* [Berkeley, 1986]) and J. B. Ross's

dark view of Italian childhood, "The Middle-Class Child in Urban Italy, Fourteenth to Early Sixteenth Century," in Lloyd DeMause, ed., *The History of Childhood* (New York, 1974), pp. 183–228.

28. Shorter, *Modern Family,* pp. 18, 99. For "hot sex" in the traditional family, see Ozment, *Flesh and Spirit,* ch. 1.

29. Jean-Louis Flandrin, *Families in Former Times: Kinship, Household, and Sexuality,* trans. Richard Southern (Cambridge, 1979), pp. 120–121, 123–124, 126, 136. Original French edition: *Familles, parenté, maison, sexualité, dans l'ancienne societé* (Paris, 1976). On the content of major confessional manuals, see Thomas N. Tentler, *Sin and Confession on the Eve of the Reformation* (Princeton, 1977).

30. Flandrin, *Families in Former Times,* pp. 118, 126–128, 137–138, 166–167, 216, 226, 235–237.

31. Ibid., p. 136.

32. Stone, *Family, Sex, and Marriage,* pp. 66, 70.

33. Ibid., p. 7–10, 55, 80, 88.

34. These characteristics developed in response to "an intolerable sense of anxiety and a deep yearning for order" caused by the loss of old religious certainties in the wake of Protestant criticism and revolt. *Ibid.,* pp. 93–94, 100, 104, 146. Stone here restates the old thesis of Keith Thomas (*Religion and the Decline of Magic* [New York, 1971]), which more recent studies have challenged. In addition to Duffy, *Stripping of the Altars,* see J. J. Scarisbrick, *The Reformation and the English People* (Oxford, 1984); and Christopher Haigh, *The English Reformation Revised* (Cambridge, 1987).

35. Stone, *Family, Sex, and Marriage,* pp. 93–94, 101, 134, 138–143, 262. Such reasons for marriage were already prominent in fifteenth-century Germany, although still secondary to the material (social and financial)

and biblical ones (propagation and a remedy to fornication). Beer, *Eltern und Kinder*, pp. 81–96; Harrington, *Reordering Marriage and Society*, p. 67.

36. Stone, *Family, Sex, and Marriage*, pp. 115, 124. "More children were beaten [in both home and school] in the sixteenth and seventeenth centuries over a longer age span than ever before"; the Protestant wife and mother "understood it to be her duty to assist her husband in . . . the repression of their children." Ibid., pp. 117, 124–126.

37. Ibid., pp. 150–152, 159–160, 180.

38. Ibid., pp. 149, 160, 169, 217–220. On Stone's stages of affection, see Alan MacFarlane, review, in *History and Theory* 19 (1980): 107.

39. Stone, *Family, Sex, and Marriage*, pp. 269, 272–274, 279, 284.

40. Stone, "Massacre of the Innocents," 25–31.

41. Robert Wheaton, "Recent Trends in the Historical Study of the French Family," in Robert Wheaton and Tamara K. Hareven, eds., *Family and Sexuality in French History* (Philadelphia, 1980), pp. 3–26. Of Stone's many critics, see especially Ralph Houlbrooke, *The English Family, 1450–1700* (London, 1984), backed up by Houlbrooke, ed., *English Family Life, 1576–1716: An Anthology from Diaries* (New York, 1988); Keith Wrightson, *English Society, 1580–1680* (New Brunswick, N.J., 1982); and, most recently, Ben-Amos, *Adolescence and Youth in Early Modern England*. See the similar criticism of Simon Schama's claim that the Dutch of the seventeenth century were the first to approach children in a modern, loving way. J. J. H. Dekker and L. F. Groenedijk, "The Republic of God or the Republic of Children? Childhood and Child-Rearing after the Reformation: An Appraisal of Simon Schama's Thesis about the Uniqueness of the Dutch Case," *Oxford Review of Education* 17 (1991): 317–335.

42. See Paul G. Spagnoli, "Philippe Ariès, Historian of the Family," *Journal of Family History* 6 (1981): 434–441.

2. A GENDERED VIEW OF FAMILY LIFE

1. A foundational study was Joan Kelly-Gadol's famous question: "Was There a Renaissance for Women?" in Renate Bridenthal et al., eds., *Becoming Visible: Women in European History* (Boston, 1977), pp. 175–202. For an updating of this question, see Judith Bennett, "History that Stands Still: Women and Work in the European Past," *Feminist Studies* 14 (1988): 269–283, and Christiane Eifert et al., eds., *Was sind Frauen? Was sind Männer? Geschlechten-Konstruktionen im historischen Wandel* (Frankfurt am Main, 1996). For the torrent of bibliography released on that question for the Renaissance and Reformation, see Merry Wiesner-Hanks, *Women and Gender in Early Modern Europe* (Cambridge, 1993) and "Family, Household, and Community," in T. A. Brady, Jr., et al., eds., *Handbook of European History 1400–1600* (Leiden, 1994), pp. 79–112; and Olwen Hufton's bibliographic essay in *The Prospect before Her: A History of Women in Western Europe, vol. 1, 1500–1800* (New York, 1996), pp. 565–613.

2. Barbara Beuys, *Familienleben in Deutschland: Neue Bilder aus der deutschen Vergangenheit* (Reinbeck bei Hamburg, 1980), p. 11.

3. Davis, "City Women and Religious Change in Sixteenth Century France," in Dorothy G. McGuigan, ed., *A Sampler of Women's Studies* (Ann Arbor, 1973), pp. 35–37.

4. Beuys, *Familienleben in Deutschland*, pp. 150–152; David Herlihy, *Opera Mulierum: Women and Work in Medieval Europe* (Cambridge, 1990), pp. 142–150; Erika Uitz, "Die Frau im Berufsleben der spätmittelalterlichen Stadt, untersucht am Beispiel von Städten auf dem Gebiet der DDR," in

Institut für mittelalterliche Realienkunde Oesterreichs, ed., *Frau und spätmittelalterlicher Alltag: Internationaler Kongress Krems an der Donau 2. bis 5. Oktober 1984* (Vienna, 1986), pp. 439–473. "In the cities of the high Middle Agres women were generally excluded from no trade for which they possessed the requisite skills." Gabriele Becker et al., eds., *"Aus der Zeit der Verzweiflung": Zur Genese und Aktualität des Hexenbildes* (Frankfurt am Main, 1977), pp. 63–64..

5. Between 1437 and 1504, 116 silk makers operated shops and trained 765 apprentices. Anke Wolf-Graaf, *Die verborgene Geschichte der Frauenarbeit. Eine Bildchronik* (Weinheim and Basel, 1983), pp. 47–49.

6. Wolf-Graaf, *Verborgene Geschichte*, p. 30. On Jewish women medical practitioners, see Joseph Shatzmiller, *Jews, Medicine, and Medieval Society* (Berkeley, 1994); on women artists, see Walter Schuchardt, *Weibliche Handwerkkunst im deutschen Mittelalters* (Berlin, 1941).

7. Beuys, *Familienleben in Deutschland*, pp. 59, 159, 162.

8. Ibid., pp. 201–202; Johannes Asen, "Die Beginen in Köln," in *Zahlreich wie die Sterne des Himmels: Beginen am Niderrhein zwischen Mythos und Wirklichkeit* (Bensberg, 1992), pp. 133–170.

9. Wolf-Graaf, *Verborgene Geschichte*, p. 52. The magisterial study of the late medieval women movements is Herbert Grundmann, *Religiose Bewegungen im Mittelalter* (Hildesheim, 1961); English: *Religious Movements in the Middle Ages*, trans. Steven Rowan (South Bend, 1995). See also Brenda Bolton, "Mulieres Sanctae," in Susan M. Stuard, ed., *Women in Medieval Society* (Philadelphia, 1976), pp. 141–158. For a comparison of the workaday lives of peasant, urban, and aristocratic women, see Henrietta Leyser, *Medieval Women: A Social History of Women in England, 450–1500* (London, 1995), pp. 142–167.

10. See especially Heide Wunder, *"Er ist die Sonn', sie ist der Mond"*: *Frauen in der Frühen Neuzeit* (Munich, 1992), pp. 75–76, 104–105. As Eileen Power pointed out in the 1920s, gender discrimination decreases as one moves from literature and theology to law and real life. *Medieval Women* (London, 1924; rpt., 1986), pp. 118–119.

11. A point stressed by Wunder, *"Er ist die Sonn', "* pp. 99–100.

12. Gernot Kocher, "Die Frau in spätmittelalterlichen Rechtsleben," in *Frau und Spätmittelalterlicher Alltag*, pp. 480–481. For a widow's purchase of citizenship, see the example of Anna Büschler in Steven Ozment, *The Bürgermeister's Daughter: Scandal in a Sixteenth-Century German Town* (New York, 1996), ch. 5.

13. Kocher, "Die Frau in spätmittelalterlichen Rechtsleben," pp. 478–481; Peter Ketsch, *Frauen im Mittelalter: Frauenbild und Frauenrechte in Kirche und Gesellschaft: Quellen und Materialen* (Düsseldorf, 1984), vol. 2, pp. 161–194.

14. Ketsch, *Frauen im Mittelalter*, vol. 2, pp. 165, 174–77. Under the proper circumstances, the earlier *Sachsenspiegel* permitted a guardian to duel the accused on behalf of his ward. Ibid., p. 168.

15. Ibid., p. 179; Kocher, "Die Frau in spätmittelalterlichen Rechtsleben," pp. 482–485; Gerhard Köbler, "Das Familienrecht in der spätmittelalterlichen Stadt," in Alfred Haverkamp, ed., *Haus und Familien der spätmittelalterlichen Stadt* (Köln, 1984), p. 156.

16. Ketsch, *Frauen im Mittelalter*, vol. 2, pp. 179–180; Becker, *"Aus der Zeit der Verzweiflung,"* p. 52.

17. Although the majority of late medieval courts recognized the competence of working women, some major German commercial centers (e.g., Regensburg and Magdeburg) continued to circumscribe working women's legal rights in court. Köbler, "Das Familienrecht in der spätmittelalterlichen

Stadt," p. 156. Generally, there is no unified treatment of women in medieval law. "The spectrum runs from abject subordination of women through gender guardianship, through relaxations of this personal form of legal authority to independent standing for a woman at work and at law." Kocher, "Die Frau im mittelalterlichen Rechtsleben," p. 485.

18. "Dennoch bot schon damals die 'Berufstätigkeit' der Frau einen ersten Ansatzpunkt für ihre Befreiung von der männlichen Vorherrschaft." Becker, *"Aus der Zeit der Verzweiflung,"* p. 49.

19. Beuys, *Familienleben in Deutschland*, p. 157; Merry E. Wiesner, *Working Women in Renaissance Germany* (New Brunswick, 1986). Wiesner especially stresses larger economic forces as she samples working women in the health professions, public service, domestic work, carnal services (bath attendants and prostitutes), and the food industries of six large German cities, finding women's forced retreat greatest in the guilds.

20. Heide Wunder, *"Er ist die Sonn',"* pp. 107–111.

21. Wolf-Graaf, *Verborgene Geschichte*, pp. 72, 81–82.

22. Ibid., p. 72; Becker, *"Aus der Zeit der Verzweiflung,"* p. 79.

23. Wunder, *"Er ist die Sonn',"* pp. 21, 23–24, 107–111.

24. The best-known example is Caritas Pirckheimer and her convent of St. Clara's in Nürnberg: *Caritas Pirckheimer, 1467–1532: Eine Ausstellung der katholischen Stadtkirche Nürnberg 26 Juni–8 August 1982* (Munich, 1982). For examples of both happy and unhappy cloister exits, see Steven Ozment, *When Fathers Ruled: Family Life in Reformation Europe* (Cambridge, Mass., 1983), pp. 9–25. On the military activities of sectarian women, see Marion Kobelt-Groch, *Aufsässige Töchter Gottes. Frauen im Bauernkrieg und in den Täuferbewegungen* (Frankfurt am Main, 1993).

25. *"Er ist die Sonn',"* pp. 94–96, 267–268.

26. "The more developed a transregional body public, the official administration of law, and institutionalized knowledge, the more woman was cast in the role of an outsider." Becker, *"Aus der Zeit der Verzweiflung,"* p. 79; Allison P. Coudert, "The Myth of the Improved Status of Protestant Women: The Case of the Witchcraze," in Jean R. Brink et al., eds. *The Politics of Gender in Early Modern Europe* (Kirksville, Mo., 1989), pp. 61–90. Lyndal Roper credits the Reformation with sanctioning the commercial status quo and attendant gender prejudices of sixteenth century small burgher households. *The Holy Household: Religion, Morals, and Order in Reformation Europe* (Oxford, 1989).

27. Hufton, *The Prospect before Her,* pp. 369–37, passim; Roper, *Holy Household;* Davis, "City Women and Religious Change," pp. 35–37; Courdert, "Myth of Improved Status," and other essays in Brink et al., eds., *Politics of Gender.* Scott Hendrix has attempted to counter the harsh portrayal of males by calling attention to the burdens of patriarchy and the existence of kinder and gentler housefathers ("Masculinity and Patriarchy"), while Sherrin Marshall has pointed out the tendentious feminism of Roper's work: *Journal of Modern History* 65 (1993): 887–889.

28. "The family as the nucleus of the state is born with this Protestant doctrine of marriage. It is Martin Luther who created on paper the family as it would centuries later come under fire: unconditionally patriarchal and authoritarian." Beuys, *Familienleben in Deutschland,* pp. 231–234; "Luther's concept of marriage is patriarchal; he relies always strongly on the traditional misogynous story of [Adam and Eve's] Fall and defines woman's role in life largely in terms of her biological function." Barbara Becker-Cantarino, *Der Lange Weg zur Mündigkeit: Frau und Literatur (1500–1800)* (Stuttgart, 1987), p. 42. Gerald Strauss has rolled several logs onto this fire:

Luther's House of Learning: Indoctrination of the Young in the German Reformation (Baltimore, 1978), pp. 169, 239–241, and *Law, Resistance, and the State: The Opposition to Roman Law in Reformation Germany* (Princeton, 1986), ch. 4. On the alleged rise and triumph of unbridled patriarchy and misogyny throughout Tudor England as well, see Anthony Fletcher, *Gender, Sex, and Subordination in England, 1500–1800* (New Haven, 1996).

29. Even Heide Wunder can detect new "hierarchies of state and household" accompanying the modern cameraderie and sharing of household authority between husband and wife in the Lutheran family, going so far as to describe the husband as "the ruler's contact" on the homefront, as if heads of household and state conspired against women at home and in society generally. *"Er ist die Sonn',"* pp. 74–75. Later, she retreats from such unconvincing conspiratorial theory. Ibid., pp. 94–95. For a kinder and more accurate description of Lutheran domestic law and practice, see John Witte, Jr., "The Transformation of Marriage Law in the Lutheran Reformation," in Witte et al., eds., *The Weightier Matters of the Law: Essays on Law and Religion* (Atlanta, 1988), pp. 57–98, and *From Sacrament to Contract: Marriage, Religion, and Law in the Western Tradition* (Louisville, 1997), ch. 2.

30. Beuys, *Familienleben in Deutschland*, p. 237; Harrington, *Reordering Marriage and Society in Reformation Germany*, p. 82; Heiko A. Oberman, *Luther: Man between God and the Devil* (New Haven, 1989), ch. 10; Ozment, *When Fathers Ruled*, pp. 98–99, and *Protestants: The Birth of a Revolution* (New York, 1992), ch. 7.

31. Beuys, *Familienleben in Deutschland*, pp. 224–225. On von Bora, see Jeanette C. Smith, "Katherina von Bora through Five Centuries: A Historiography," *Sixteenth-Century Journal* 30 (1999): 745–774, and Martin Treu, *Katherine von Bora* (Wittenberg, 1995). On other successful Protestant

women, see Roland Bainton, *Women of the Reformation in Germany and Italy* (Minneapolis, 1971); and Barbara Becker-Cantarino, "Frauen in den Glaubenskämpfen. Oeffentliche Briefe, Lieder und Gelegenheitsschriften," in Gisela Brinker-Gabler, ed., *Deutsche Literatur von Frauen*, vol. 1: *Vom Mittelalter bis zum Ende des 18. Jahrhunderts* (Munich, 1988), pp. 149–171. On the worldly activities of Anabaptist and peasant women, see Kobelt-Groch, *Aufsässige Töchter*.

32. What Wunder calls "putting the family at the center of work and life." *"Er ist die Sonn',"* pp. 267–268; ch. 4.

33. On the late marriage pattern in western Europe: J. Hajnal, "European Marriage Patterns in Perspective," in D. V. Glass and D. E. C. Eversley, eds., *Population in History* (Chicago, 1965).

34. Steven Ozment, *The Age of Reform, 1250–1550: An Intellectual and Religious History of Late Medieval and Reformation Europe* (New Haven, 1980), ch. 12, pp. 381–396, 378 (Zwingli); August Franzen, *Zölibat und Priesterehe in der Auseinandersetzung der Reformationszeit und der katholischen Reform des 16. Jahrhundert* (Paderborn, 1969).

35. Wunder, *"Er ist die Sonn',"* pp. 59–63; Ozment, *When Fathers Ruled*, pp. 3–9.

36. Witte, *From Sacrament to Contract*, ch. 2.

37. *Luthers Werke in Auswahl*, vol. 8, *Tischreden*, ed. Otto Clemen (Berlin, 1950) (henceforth *Tischreden*), no. 7 (1531), p. 1; John Witte, Jr., "The Civic Seminar: Sources of Modern Public Education in the Lutheran Reformation of Germany," *Journal of Law and Religion* 12 (1995–96): 188, n 71.

38. *Luther: Letters of Spiritual Counsel*, ed. and trans. T. G. Tappert (Philadephia [1955]), pp. 291–294.

39. Wunder, *"Er ist die Sonn'*, *"* pp. 67–69, and, less decisively, Harrington, *Reordering Marriage and Society,* pp. 164–166; Bruce Boehner, "Early Modern Syphilis," *Journal of the History of Sexuality* 1 (1990): 197–214; W. Schlerner, "Moral Attitudes toward Syphilis and Its Prevention in the Renaissance," *Bulletin of Medical History* 68 (1994): 389–410.

40. On those portrayals, see Ian MacLean, *The Renaissance Notion of Woman: A Study in the Fortunes of Scholasticism and Medical Science in European Intellectual Life* (Cambridge, 1980); and Vern Bullough, "Medieval Medical and Scientific Views of Women," *Viator* 4 (1973): 485–501.

41. *Tischreden,* no. 4910 (1540), p. 244; no. 5189 (1540), p. 275; Oberman, *Luther,* pp. 277–283. According to Wunder, Luther viewed his wife as a "Gefährtin," not "Gehilfin," a "companion and comrade," not an "assistant." *"Er ist die Sonn',"* p. 73; Ozment, *When Fathers Ruled,* ch. 1; Hendrix, "Masculinity and Patriarchy in Reformation Germany.".

42. "I appoint you, Katie, as universal heiress. You bore the children and gave them your breast. You will not manage their affairs to their disadvantage. I am hostile to guardians, who seldom do things correctly." *Tischreden,* no. 5041 (1540), cited in *Luther's Works,* vol. 34, ed. Lewis W. Spitz (Philadelphia, 1960), pp. 291–292, preface to "Luther's Will." See also H. G. Haile, *Luther* (New York, 1980), p. 271; Martin Brecht, *Martin Luther,* vol. 3: *The Preservation of the Church 1532–1546,* trans. James L. Schaaf (Philadelphia, 1985), pp. 243–244.

43. Wunder, *"Er ist die Sonn'*, *"* pp. 64–65, 70; Ozment, *When Fathers Ruled,* pp. 80–99; and Witte, "Transformation of Marriage Law," pp. 57–97, and *From Sacrament to Contract,* ch. 3. For individual cases: Thomas Max Safley, *Let No Man Put Asunder: The Control of Marriage in the German Southwest, 1550–1600* (Kirksville, Mo., 1984) (Protestant Basel); Adrian

Staehelin, *Die Einführung der Ehescheidung in Basel zur Zeit der Reformation* (Basel, 1957); Hartweg Dieterich, *Das Protestantische Eherecht in Deutschland bis zur Mitte des 17. Jahrhunderts* (Munich, 1970); Judith W. Harvey, "The Influence of the Reformation on Nürnberg Marriage Laws, 1520–1535" (Ph.D. diss., Ohio State University, 1972).

44. Wunder, *"Er ist die Sonn','"* pp. 73, 267.

45. See Pope Innocent III's (1198–1216) famous declaration and its elaboration by papal pamphleteers in Brian Tierney, *The Crisis of Church and State, 1050–1300* (Englewood Cliffs, 1964), pp. 131–132, and *Origins of Papal Infallibility: 1150–1350* (Leiden, 1972); Ozment, *Age of Reform,* pp. 144–155.

46. Wunder elaborates the relationship as "fundamentally unequal," yet lacking any "general subordination"—a "reciprocal" relationship, in which the "equal worth" of each is recognized. *"Er ist die Sonn','"* pp. 265, 267.

47. Ibid., pp. 267–268.

48. Ibid., pp. 107–111.

49. Ibid., pp. 75–76; Ozment, *When Fathers Ruled,* pp. 9–24.

50. Ben-Amos, *Adolescence and Youth in Early Modern England,* pp. 145, 155.

51. Wunder, *"Er ist die Sonn','"* pp. 99–102, 104–105.

52. Ibid., p. 114; see the example of Magdalena Römer Behaim in Ozment, *Three Behaim Boys,* pp. 93–160; *Flesh and Spirit,* ch. 3.

53. For the two ends of the spectrum on this subject and the historiographical traditions in between, see Strauss, *Law, Resistance, and the State,* ch. 7 (esp. pp. 238–239), and Ozment, *Protestants,* ch. 6 ("Luther's Political Legacy").

54. Wunder, *"Er ist die Sonn','"* p. 74.

55. "Ansprechspartner der Obrigkeiten." Ibid., p. 75.

56. As Wunder herself points out, saving herself from an uncharacteristic lapse into unconvincing conspiracy theory. Ibid., pp. 94–95. On the primacy of familial priorities in the sixteenth century household, see Ozment, *Flesh and Spirit,* Introduction and Conclusion.

57. Ozment, *Protestants,* chs. 3, 6; Fichtner, *Primogeniture and Protestantism.* Cf. Thomas A. Brady, Jr., *Protestant. Politics: Jacob Sturm and the German Reformation* (Atlantic Highlands, N.J., 1995).

58. Cf. Heide Wunder, "Ueberlegungen zum 'Modernisierungschub des historischen Denkens im 18. Jahrhundert' aus der Perspektive der Geschlechtergeschichte," in W. Küttler et al., eds., *Geschichtsdiskurs,* vol. 2: *Anfänge modernen historischen Denkens* (Frankfurt am Main, 1994), pp. 320–332.

3. REBUILDING THE PREMODERN FAMILY

1. Contrary to Lawrence Stone, Alan MacFarlane claims to find "companionate marriages" based on "mutual society, help, and comfort" firmly in place as early as 1300, indeed, "as far back as we can easily go." *Marriage and Love in England, 1300–1840* (Oxford, 1986), pp. 124, 183, 321–322. That argument is made today by numerous family historians in other national traditions as well.

2. Various of these sources, but particularly proverbs and songs, were exploited in the popular French series *A History of Private Life,* vols. 1–5, ed. Philippe Ariès and Georges Duby, trans. Arthur Goldhammer (Cambridge, Mass., 1987–1991). On mining the comparatively silent centuries and social groups, see Hanawalt, *Growing Up in Medieval London,* chs. 1, 2; Peter Burke, *Popular Culture in Early Modern Europe* (New York, 1978), pp. 68–77; Dülmen, *Kultur und Alltag,* pp. 56–77.

3. Suzanne Dixon, *The Roman Family* (Baltimore, 1992), pp. 74–75.

4. Ibid., pp. 83–96; Herlihy, *Medieval Households,* pp. 9–10, 15; Susan Treggiari, *Roman Marriage: Lusti Coniuges from the Time of Cicero to the Time of Ulpian* (Oxford, 1991).

5. Herlihy, *Medieval Households,* pp. 15–23, and *Opera Muliebria,* ch. 1.

6. Herlihy, *Medieval Households,* pp. 82–95.

7. Among German sources, the diverse biographies of Hildegard of Bingen (1098–1179) and Landgravine Elisabeth of Thuringia (1207–1231), both of whom were destined to become saints, are routinely cited as evidence that women in the Middle Ages knew a great deal about human sexuality (Hildegard) and physical love and gave themselves over to them enthusiastically (Elisabeth). Beuys, *Familienleben in Deutschland,* p. 193; Alfred Havekamp, ed., *Hildegard von Bingen in ihrem historischen Umfeld* (Mainz, 1999).

8. Herlihy, *Medieval Households,* pp. 115, 118–119, 129. Shulamith Shahar's recent survey of medieval childhood relies heavily on such sources to reconstruct a balanced history of children. *Childhood in the Middle Ages,* trans. Chaya Galai (London, 1992). On the resources in miracle stories, see Ronald C. Finucane, *The Rescue of the Innocents: Endangered Children in Medieval Miracles* (New York, 1997), and Michael Goodich, *Violence and Miracle in the Fourteenth Century* (Chicago, 1994).

9. Dülmen, *Kultur und Alltag in der Frühen Neuzeit,* pp. 43–45.

10. For examples of burgher wives active in their husband's businesses: Steven Ozment, *Magdalena and Balthasar; An Intimate Portrait of Life in Sixteenth-Century Europe Revealed in the Letters of a Nuremberg Husband and*

Wife (New York, 1986); Shulamith Shahar, *The Fourth Estate: A History of Women in the Middle Ages* (London, 1983), chs. 5, pp. 126–173, and 6, esp. pp. 189–203. On the education and opportunities of noblewomen: Beuys, *Familienleben in Deutschland,* pp. 175–178, 186–187; Heide Wunder, "'Gewirkte Geschichte': Gedenken und 'Handarbeit': Ueberlegungen zum Tradieren von Geschichte im Mittelalter und zu seinem Wandel am Beginn der Neuzeit," in Joachim Heinzle, ed., *Modernes Mittelalter: Neue Bilder einer populären Epoche* (Frankfurt, am Main, 1994), pp. 324–354. For what a noblewoman might accomplish politically on her family's behalf by virtue of her high position and charm, see Wunder, *"Er ist die Sonn',"* p. 221, and Hufton, *The Prospect before Her,* ch. 4, who searches out the more negative aspects.

11. Ariès, *Centuries of Childhood,* p. 413.

12. Jean-Louis Flandrin, "Contraception, Marriage, and Sexual Relations in the Christian West," in Robert Forster and Orest Renum, eds., *Biology of Man in History: Selections from the Annales,* vol. 1 (Baltimore, 1975), p. 45; Flandrin, *Families in Former Times,* pp. 216–217, 224–226, 235–237.

13. John T. Noonan, *Contraception: A History of Its Treatment by the Catholic Theologians and Canonists* (New York, 1965), pp. 79–94, 138–160, 221–236; Emmanuel La Roy Ladurie, *Montaillou: The Promised Land of Error* (New York, 1978), which devotes considerable attention to Cathar sexuality.

14. Claudia Opitz, "Zwischen Fluch und Heiligkeit—kinderlose Frauen im späteren Mittelalter," in Barbara Neuwirth, ed., *Frauen, die sich keine Kinder wünschen* (Wien, 1988), pp. 84, 109–110; Shahar, *Childhood in the Middle Ages,* pp. 36–37; Ozment, *Flesh and Spirit,* ch. 2.

15. Opitz, "Zwischen Fluch und Heiligkeit," pp. 105, 111. On the many imaginative things religious women could do within the limited world of the cloister, see Caroline W. Bynum, *Holy Feast, Holy Fast: The Religious Significance of Food to Medieval Women* (New York, 1987).

16. The most comprehensive account is still Noonan, *Contraception*. Succinct summaries in P. P. A. Biller, "Birth-Control in the West in the Thirteenth and Early Fourteenth Centuries," *Past and Present* 94 (1982): 22; Klaus Arnold, *Kind und Gesellschaft in Mittelalter und Renaissance* (Paderborn, 1980), pp. 55, 57; Emmanuel Le Roy Ladurie, *Montaillou* (Paris, 1975; English ed., trans. Barbara Bray (London, 1978), pp. 172–174. Biller, in his discussion of "appreciable contraception," especially challenges the "minimalist" views of Noonan and Flandrin, citing prostitutes, single people in illicit relationships, and married couples determined to space pregnancies. "Birth-Control," 25.

17. Noonan, *Contraception*, p. 227, n. 47, cited by Biller, "Birth-Control," 24; Arnold, *Kind und Gesellschaft*, pp. 54–55.

18. Arnold, *Kind und Gesellschaft*, pp. 55–56. Biller cites David Herlihy's early studies of Pistoia (1965), Florence (1969, 1970), and Verona (1973) ("Birth-Control," 6), to which should be added Herlihy's masterpiece, with Christiane Klapisch-Zuber, *Tuscans and Their Families*. "At the very least the demographic figures of the fourteenth and fifteenth centuries suggest that population control, in forms acceptable or unacceptable to the Church, occurred." Noonan, *Contraception*, p. 280.

19. Thomas Tentler, *Sin and Confession and Confession on the Eve of the Reformation* (Princeton, 1977), pp. 174–186, 224–226.

20. Biller, "Birth-Control:" 15–17; Opitz, "Zwischen Fluch und Heiligkeit," p. 90; James Brundage, "Carnal Delight: Canonistic Theories

of Sexuality," in Stephan Kuttner and Kenneth Pennington, eds., *Proceedings of the Fifth International Congress of Medieval Canon Law, Salamanca, 21–25 September 1976* (Vatican City, 1980), pp. 364–367, 383.

4. THE OMNIPRESENT CHILD

1. "The Evolution of Childhood," in Lloyd DeMause, ed., *The History of Childhood: The Untold Story of Child Abuse* (New York, 1974), p. 1. The four intermediate stages are abandonment (fourth to thirteenth centuries), ambivalence (fourteenth to seventeenth), intrusiveness (eighteenth), and socialization (nineteenth to twentieth). Ibid., pp. 51–54. In one instance, a recent study finds children, not parents, to be autonomous "little monsters," as they freely make accusations that place adults, including their parents, at the stake. Wolfgang Behringer, "Kinderhexenprozesse: Zur Rolle von Kindern in der Geschichte der Hexenverfolgung," *Zeitschrift für Historische Forschung* 16 (1989): 31–47. On this subject, see also Hartwig Weber, *Kinderhexenprozesse* (Frankfurt am Main, 1991) and Paul Boyer and Stephan Nissenbaum, *Salem Possessed: The Social Origins of Witchcraft* (Cambridge, Mass., 1974).

2. *Children and Childhood in Western Society Since 1500* (London, 1995), pp. 47, 56.

3. In addition to Beer's works cited above, see the analysis of Michael Borgolte, "Familienforschung und Geschlechtergeschichte," in *Sozialgeschichte des Mittelalters. Eine Forschungsbilanz nach der deutschen Einheit* (Munich, 1996), pp. 385–444, with an extensive bibliography of works since 1950.

4. Cunningham's most immediate source is Philip Greven's study of the "Protestant temperament" in colonial America, *The Protestant Tempera-*

ment: *Patterns of Child-Rearing, Religious Experience, and the Self in Early America* (New York, 1977); Cunningham, *Children and Childhood*, p. 56. For in-depth studies of parental and child behavior within specific Protestant families, cf. particularly the cited works of Mathias Beer, Alfred Haverkamp, and Steven Ozment.

5. The comparison is Shahar's, *Childhood in the Middle Ages*, pp. 20–21, ch. 2.

6. Arnold, *Kind und Gesellschaft*, p. 17.

7. Shahar cites evidence of contemporary authorities extending adolescence to twenty-eight, thirty, and even thirty-five years of age. *Childhood in the Middle Ages*, p. 28. On the stages of woman's life according to fifteenth- and sixteenth-century authors, see Wunder, *"Er ist die Sonn',"* ch. 2.

8. Shahar, *Childhood in the Middle Ages*, pp. 21–22; Arnold, *Kind und Gesellschaft*, pp. 18–20; Luke DeMaitre, "The Idea of Childhood and Child Care in Medical Writings of the Middle Ages," *Journal of Psychohistory* 4 (1976–1977): 461–490; 465. Another indirect, but pregnant source for knowledge of childhood are the many surviving literary texts of the High Middle Ages, comprehensively and penetratingly treated for Germany by James A. Schultz, *The Knowledge of Childhood in the German Middle Ages, 1100–1350* (Philadelphia, 1995).

9. Arnold, *Kind und Gesellschaft*, p. 86; Wunder, *"Er ist die Sonn',"* p. 59.

10. M. M. McLaughlin, "Survivors and Surrogates, Ninth to Thirteenth Centuries," in DeMause, *History of Childhood*, pp. 101–181: p. 140.

11. David Herlihy, "Medieval Children," in Steven Ozment and Frank M. Turner, eds., *The Many Sides of History*, vol. 1 (New York, 1987), pp. 155–173.

12. The church is that of St. Madeleine of Vézelay (1125–1140). Arnold, *Kind und Gesellschaft*, pp. 30–31, with illustration.

13. For Spain, see William Christian, Jr., *Apparitions in Late Medieval and Renaissance Spain* (Princeton, 1981), and Carlos M. N. Eire, *From Madrid to Purgatory: The Art and Craft of Dying in Sixteenth-Century Spain* (Cambridge, 1995); for England, Jonathan Sumption, *Pilgrimage: An Image of Medieval Religion* (London, 1975); and for Germany, Lionel Rothkrug, *Religious Practices and Collective Perceptions: Hidden Homologies in the Renaissance and Reformation* (Waterloo, Ontario, 1980).

14. See the example of parents Christoph and Katharina Scheurl in 1530s Nürnberg, who had to bear four nonviable early births and six stillborn infants carried to term before producing two surviving sons. Ozment, *Flesh and Spirit*, ch. 2.

15. Examples from Arnold, in criticism of Edward Shorter, in *Kind und Gesellschaft*, pp. 31–37. Citing the 1468 example of a Nürnberg butcher who turned his knife on himself after losing his two children in a fire, Arnold insists that parents in the past also had the "ability to grieve." See also Shahar, *Childhood in the Middle Ages*, pp. 147, 150–151. Historians also note the heroic examples of parents, particularly fathers, who continued to care for their children under impossible economic and hygienic conditions: "erstaunliche Einsatzbereitschaft für das Wohl ihrer Kinder." Van Dülmen, *Kultur und Alltag in Frühen Neuzeit*, pp. 96, 98, 106.

16. Beer, *Eltern und Kinder*, pp. 207, 225, 238, 248–250, 261, 268–270, and "Kinder in den Familien deutscher Städte des späten Mittelalters und der frühen Neuzeit," *Zeitschrift für Kulturwissenschaften* 6 (1994): 25–48; Hans Boesch, *Kinderleben in der deutschen Vergangenheit . . . 15.–18. Jahrhundert*

(Leipzig, 1900; rpt. Düsseldorf, 1979), pp. 38–45; Ozment, *Magdalena and Balthasar,* ch. 4, and *Flesh and Spirit,* ch. 2.

17. "Many a father's and also a mother's heart was stricken with great fear." Historischer Verein des Kantons St. Gallen, ed., *Sabbata: Mit kleineren Schriften und Briefen* (St. Gall, 1902), Book 7, p. 445, lines 16–31; cf. Beer, *Eltern und Kinder,* p. 283. On Kessler's career, see E. Gorden Rupp, *Patterns of Reformation* (Philadephia, 1969), pp. 357–378.

18. Opitz, "Zwischen Fluch und Heiligkeit," pp. 90–91; Arnold, *Kind und Gesellschaft,* p. 53. Emily R. Coleman suspects that premeditated murder of female children at birth—for understandable economic reasons— explains the gender disproportion she finds in the seigneurial census roll of Saint-Germain-des-Pres ("L'infanticide dans le haut Moyen Age," *Annales ESC* 29 [1974]: 315–335), a conclusion for which Arnold (in *Kind und Gesellschaft*) claims she lacks reliable data. Shahar recognizes some criminal negligence, yet believes most reported accidents were truly such. *History of Childhood in the Middle Ages,* pp. 131, 139–144.

19. These Church measures are found in pentitential books and canonical commentaries used to train parish priests, as well as in rulings of the diocesan synods that applied church doctrine and law. In secular law, premeditated infanticide and child murder were capital crimes punished by drowning, burning, and burial alive. Arnold, *Kind und Gesellschaft,* pp. 46–52; Shahar, *Childhood in the Middle Ages,* pp. 131, 139–140. On the problems of documenting abandonment and infanticide, especially in earlier historical periods, and the evidence of positive parental attitudes there, see Peter Garnsey, "Child-Rearing in Ancient Italy," in D. Kertzer and R. Saller, eds., *The Family in Italy: Antiquity to the Present* (New Haven, 1991), pp. 48–65.

20. Arnold, *Kind und Gesellschaft*, pp. 60–62; Herlihy, *Medieval House-holds*, pp. 132–134, and "The Making of the Medieval Family: Symmetry, Structure, and Sentiment," *Journal of Family History* 2 (1983): 116–130.

21. Arnold, *Kind und Gesellschaft*, p. 48.

22. Ibid., p. 53.

23. Hanawalt, *Growing Up in Medieval London*, p. 44. Ulinka Rublack addresses the punishment of infanticide in early modern Germany, where the crime was unforgivable and executions (beheading) common when the case was airtight—an indication of "how much motherly aggression [then] went against the construction of good motherhood." *The Crimes of Women in Early Modern Germany* (Oxford, 1999), p. 165.

24. Arnold cites 1980s statistics for (then) West Germany, and Shahar more recent ones for the United States. *Kind und Gesellschaft*, p. 43; *Childhood in the Middle Ages*, pp. 110, 173.

25. *Young Man Luther* (New York, 1962); *Childhood and Society* (New York, 1963); *Ghandi's Truth on the Origins of Militant Nonviolence* (New York, 1969). Frank J. Sulloway bounces imaginatively from century to century and from professional field to professional field testing a similarly derived hypothesis about birth order and rebelliousness. *Born to Rebel: Birth Order, Family Dynamics, and Creative Lives* (New York, 1996). On the reactions of historians to Erikson, see Roger A. Johnson, ed., *Psychohistory and Religion: The Case of "Young Man Luther"* (Philadelphia, 1977).

26. Thus, Rudolf Lenz, "Emotion und Affektion in der Familie in der Frühen Neuzeit: Leichenpredigten als Quellen der Historischer Familien-forschung," in P.-J. Schuler, ed., *Die Familie als sozialer und historischer verband* (Sigmaringen, 1987), pp. 121–146," and Hanawalt, *Growing Up in Medieval London*, pp. 5–13. See also Wunder's criticism of similarly tenden-

tious feminist readings of the centuries between 1500 and 1800. *"Er ist die Sonn',"* pp. 267–268.

27. An example of Christian's work is *Local Religion in Sixteenth Century Spain* (Princeton, 1981) and, of Davis's, *Society and Culture in Early Modern France* (Berkeley, 1975). On the disputes and problems in appropriating the theories and methods of the social sciences for the study of popular culture in the past, see especially R. W. Scribner, "Is a History of Popular Culture Possible?" *History of European Ideas* 10 (1989): 175–191, and Gerald Strauss, "Viewpoint: The Dilemma of Popular History," *Past and Present* 132 (1991): 130–149.

28. Arnold, *Kind und Gesellschaft*, pp. 49, 52.

29. Shahar, *Childhood in the Middle Ages*, pp. 85–86.

30. Beer, *Eltern und Kinder*, p. 261.

31. Both works are discussed in Ozment, *When Fathers Ruled*, pp. 116–118; on Coler and the housefather book genre, see Julius Hoffmann, *Die "Hausväterliteratur" und die "Predigten über den christlichen Hausstand": Lehre vom Hause und Bildung für das häusliche Leben im 16. 17. und 18. Jahrhundert* (Weinheim, 1959).

32. David Hunt, *Parents and Children in History: The Psychology of Family Life in Early Modern France* (New York, 1970), pp. 128–132.

33. Hufton, *The Prospect before Her*, pp. 197–202; Shahar, *Childhood in the Middle Ages*, pp. 53, 69–70, 75; Ozment, *When Fathers Ruled*, pp. 116–121. For a bibliography, see Valerie A. Fildes, *Breasts, Bottles, and Babies: A History of Infant Feeding* (Edinburgh, 1986).

34. Ozment, *Protestants*, p. 174; Shahar, *Childhood in the Middle Ages*, pp. 53–54.

35. On the successful introduction of other liquids into an infant's diet in the sixteenth-century Scheurl family, see Ozment, *Flesh and Spirit*, ch. 2.

36. J. B. Ross, "The Middle-Class Child in Urban Italy, Fourteenth to Early Sixteenth Century," p. 215.

37. "If wetnursing was common in London, we cannot trace the children or the nurses either in the countryside or in the merchant houses." Hanawalt, *Growing Up in Medieval London*, p. 56.

38. Beer, *Eltern und Kinder*, pp. 248, 250, 255.

39. The Scheurls of Nürnberg hired a widowed nurse for each of their two sons, and both women nursed in. The first had lost both husband and child, while the child of the second was apparently weaned before she entered the Scheurl household (it did not accompany her there). Ozment, *Flesh and Spirit*, ch. 2.

40. August Nitschke, "Die Stellung des Kindes in der Familie im Spätmittelalter und in der Renaissance," in Haverkamp, ed., *Haus und Familie in der spätmittelalterlichen Stadt*, pp. 215–243. Nitschke juxtaposes the fifteenth-century viewpoints of a German, Konrad von Megenberg, and an Italian, Leon Battista Alberti. The latter's famous philosophical treatise on the family is translated by Rene N. Watkins, *The Family in Renaissance Florence* [Columbia, S.C., 1962).

41. While traveling with an apparent toddling girl cousin, Magdalena Paumgartner describes her as running around the coach "like a little monkey." Ozment, *Magdalena and Balthasar*, p. 103. Christoph Scheurl frequently comments on his son's imitative behavior. Ozment, *Flesh and Spirit*, ch. 2.

42. August Nitschke, *Junge Rebellen, Mittelalter, Neuzeit, Gegenwart: Kinder verändern die Welt* (Munich, 1985), pp. 50–57. Ozment, *When Fathers Ruled*, ch. 4; Strauss, *Luther's House of Learning*, chs. 2, 3.

43. Nitschke, "Die Stellung des Kindes," pp. 242–243; Ozment, *Flesh and Spirit*, ch. 2.

44. This is illustrated, vocationally and matrimonally, in the youthful lives of Nürnbergers Michael Behaim and Stephan Carl Behaim. Ozment, *Three Behaim Boys*. See also Paul Behaim's choice of his own course of study, and Lorenz Dürnhofer's early transfer from a mercantile to a scholarly career when the former grated against his aptitude and his temperament. Ozment, *Flesh and Spirit*, chs. 3, 5. In England, "the child's approval, inclination and individual judgment were all taken into account" before he or she was placed in service. Ben-Amos, *Adolescence and Youth in Early Modern England*, pp. 63–66.

45. In addition to Nitschke ("Die Stellung des Kindes"), see Gordon Griffiths et al., *The Humanism of Leonardo Bruni and Selected Texts* (Binghamton, 1987), and William H. Woodward, *Studies in Education during the Age of the Renaissance, 1400–1600* (New York, 1967).

46. Arnold, *Kind und Gesellschaft*, pp. 60–67, 73–74; Beer, *Eltern und Kinder*, pp. 290–297; Shahar, *Childhood in the Middle Ages*, pp. 95–96, 103–105; Boesch, *Kinderleben in der deutschen Vergangenheit*, pp. 63–68, 70–72 (with contemporary sketches of toys and games); Ozment, *When Fathers Ruled*, pp. 135, 141, 155, 157. Pieter Brueghel's *Children's Games* (1560) depicts seventy-five different games: Jeanette Hills, *Das Kinderspielsbild von Pieter Brueghel der Aeltere* (Vienna, 1957).

47. Boesch, *Kinderleben in der deutschen Vergangenheit*, pp. 73–78; Arnold, *Kind und Gesellschaft*, pp. 73–76; Karl Simrock, *Das deutsche*

Kinderbuch: Alterthümliche Reime, Lieder, Erzahlungen, Uebungen, Räthsel, und Scherze für Kinder, 3rd ed. (Berlin, 1879).

48. All these examples are from Boesch, who provides many more. *Kinderleben in der deutschen Vergangenheit,* pp. 78–85.

49. Ibid., pp. 84–85.

50. Köbler, "Das Familienrecht in der spätmittelalterlichen Stadt," pp. 139, 158; Shahar, *Childhood in the Middle Ages,* pp. 113, 115.

51. Heide Wunder, "Wie wird man ein Mann? Befunde am Beginn der Neuzeut (15.–17. Jahrhundert)," in Eifert et al., *Was sind Frauen,* pp. 127–130.

52. See the guiding hand of Nürnberg widow Magdalena Römer Behaim in the lives of sons Friedrich, at school in nearby Altdorf (Ozment, *Three Behaim Boys,* pp. 92–160), and Paul, a law student in Padua (Ozment, *Flesh and Spirit,* ch. 3); also widower Lorenz Dürnhofer's devotion to educating and arranging marriages for his daughters (ibid., ch. 5). On the independent "wandering" of young women apprentices in search of skills and work, see Wunder, *"Er ist die Sonn',"* pp. 178–179.

53. Arnold, *Kind und Gesellschaft,* p. 25.

54. Examples of children's confessions are in Johannes Geffken, *Bilderkatechismus des fünfzehnten Jahrhunderts* (Leipzig, 1855), p. 25. See also Etienne Delaruelle et al., *L'Eglise au temps du Grand Schisme et de la crise conciliaire (1378–1449)* (Paris, 1964), p. 656; Peter Browe, "Die Pflichtbeichte im Mittelalter," *Zeitschrift für katholische theologie* 57 (1933): 335–383; Steven E. Ozment, *The Reformation in the Cities: The Appeal of Protestantism to Sixteenth-Century Germany and Switzerland* (New Haven, 1975), pp. 22–23.

55. Klaus Petzold, *Die Grundlagen der Erziehungslehre im Spätmittelater und bei Luther* (Heidelberg, 1969), pp. 84–89.

56. In addition to the methodical development of a child's talents, engendering obedience, diligence, and an ethical will was a priority of child rearing in the housefather books. Hoffmann, *Die "Hausväterliteratur,"* pp. 150–151. Cf. the harsher, speculative conclusion drawn from didactic literature by Strauss, *Luther's House of Learning,* pp. 239–241.

57. The housefather books approved of corporal punishment only for behavior threatening or injurious to a child. Hoffmann, *Die "Hausväterliteratur,"* p. 152. Arnold documents the many urgings of parental kindness in child rearing. *Kind und Gesellschaft,* pp. 81–83. On the recommendations of parental gentleness by reformers and humanists, see Ozment, *When Fathers Ruled,* ch. 4; on their pursuit among laity, Ozment, *Flesh and Spirit,* chs. 2, 5.

58. Thus Stone, *Family, Sex, and Marriage in England,* pp. 116–118, 124–126. Hunt generalizes from the remarkably exceptional infancy and childhood of the French king Louis XIII, who was whipped thoroughly at two years of age. *Parents and Children,* pp. 133, 135, 139, 153. Hufton and Strauss judge corporal punishment more fairly, despite their irrepressible anticlericalism. *The Prospect before Her,* pp. 211–212; *Luther's House of Learning,* pp. 180–182.

59. On the collaboration of state and religion in this process in Reformation Germany, see Witte, "Civic Seminary," 173–223.

60. Shahar, *Childhood in the Middle Ages,* pp. 225–226. Ben-Amos's sample finds English urban youths beginning apprenticeships at a mean age of 14.7; in the countryside, service did not begin before thirteen. Despite contracts extending up to seven years, many crafts and trades could be mastered in three or four, at which point the majority of apprentices usually went their own way. *Adolescence and Youth in Early Modern England,* pp. 62, 123, 130. Hanawalt finds youths in fourteenth century London entering appren-

ticeships normally at fourteen, but as late as eighteen, and between sixteen and eighteen in the fifteenth century. *Growing Up in Medieval London*, pp. 113–114, 120. Ross's calculations for Italian youths approximate Ariès's guesses at when children left the parental household (seven), finding boys at home for only five years, between the ages of two and seven (the first two years of life spent at the home of a wet nurse) before being placed at school or in an apprenticeship. Girls remained in the parental home for a longer period of time, entering convents at nine or ten or, far more often, marrying by sixteen. If generally true, these conclusions contrast sharply with German practice. Ross, "The Middle-Class Child in Urban Italy," 215–216. On German apprentices, see Kurt Wesoly, *Lehrlinge und Handwerksgesellen am Mittelrhein: Ihre soziale Lage und ihre Organization von 14. bis ins 17. Jahrhundert* (Frankfurt am Main, 1985); and Ozment, *Three Behaim Boys*, pp. 11–92.

61. "Life-cycle service was obviously complementary to, rather than a replacement of, the parental home [and] the parental bond [still] surpassed all other ties." Ben-Amos, *Adolescence and Youth in Early Modern England*, p. 165. Ben-Amos especially criticizes the historians of the 1960s and 1970s for ignoring this well-documented continuity. Ibid., pp. 4–6, 73, 159–161.

5. PARENTAL ADVICE

1. Eugen Schöler, *Fränkische Wappen erzählen Geschichte und Geschichten* (Neustadt a.d. Aisch, 1992), pp. 94–95; Jean Devisse and Michel Mollat, *The Image of the Black in Western Art*, vol. 2 (Cambridge, Mass., 1970), pp. 215–218.

2. By permission of Mathias Beer, "Private Correspondence in the Reformation Era: A Forgotten Source for the History of the Burgher Family," forthcoming in *Sixteenth Century Journal* (2001). See also Beer's magis-

terial study of Nürnberg family life for similar parent-child relationships in numerous contemporary families, including the Tuchers. *Eltern und Kinder.*

3. Friedrich Beyschlag, ed., "Ein Vater an seinen Sohn (1539)," *Archiv für Kulturgeschichte* 4 (1906): 296–302. Translated and discussed in Ozment, *Flesh and Spirit*, pp. 261–264.

4. Ralph Houlbrooke, ed., *English Family Life, 1576–1716: An Anthology from Diaries* (Oxford, 1989), p. 183. Cf. Steven Ozment, "Premodern Advice for the Postmodern Young," *The Public Interest* 119 (1995): pp. 54–67.

5. Houlbrooke, *English Family Life*, p. 184. Compare the similar handling of a wayward son in the Nürnberg Behaim family: Ozment, *Three Behaim Boys*, pp. 272–282.

6. Houlbrooke, *English Family Life*, pp. 194–195.

7. Ibid., p. 195.

8. "Ein nützliches und brauchbares Mitglied der menschlichen Gesellschaft." In Erika Hoffmann, ed., *Briefe grosser Deutscher an Kinder: Deutsche Männer schreiben an Kinder* (Berlin, 1943), no. 30, p. 62. Of the many readily available collections of such useful material, the three volumes edited by Angela and Andreas Hopf, which pull together classic German examples, may also be consulted: *Geliebtes Kind! Elternbreife aus zwölf Jahrhunderten; Geliebte Eltern! Kinderbriefe aus sechs Jahrhunderten;* and *Archiv des Herzens: Partnerbriefe aus neun Jahrhunderten* (Ismaning bei Münich, 1986, 1987, 1988).

9. In Hoffmann, *Briefe grosser Deutscher*, pp. 62–63.

10. "Eine Einfachheit, eine Gradheit, eine derbe Tüchtigkeit."

11. "Eingewickelte Leerheit."

12. "Die Blumen und Blüten abstreifen."

13. "Verdummen in leeren Formelwesen."

14. In Hoffmann, *Briefe grosser Deutscher*, no. 64, p. 194.

15. "Doch traue nicht flugs und allerdings."

16. In Hoffmann, *Briefe grosser Deutscher*, no. 37, p. 105.

17. From *The Life and Letters of Mrs. Sewell* (London, 1889), cited in Linda Pollock, ed., *A Lasting Relationship: Parents and Children over Three Centuries* (London, 1987), p. 220.

18. In Hoffmann, *Briefe grosser Deutscher*, no. 50, pp. 143–144.

19. Which committed him to grow into the commandments of God.

20. "Mich in Dir einmal glücklich zu sehen."

21. Revelation 9:11: "They have as king over them the angel of the bottomless pit; his name in Hebrew is Abaddon, and in Greek he is called Apollyon," meaning "destroyer."

22. September 9, 1783. In Hoffmann, *Briefe Grosser Deutscher*, no. 36, pp. 93–95.

23. Compare Stephan Carl Behaim, in Ozment, *Three Behaim Boys*, pp. 227–282.

24. October 1, 1832. In Hoffmann, ed., *Briefe Grosser Deutscher*, no. 69, pp. 210–211.

25. Ibid.

26. October 28, 1621. In *ibid.*, no. 7, pp. 19–20. See also Balthasar Paumgartner's alternate use of threats, promises, and gifts to encourage good behavior in his son, Balthasar, Jr. Ozment, *Magdalena and Balthasar*, ch. 4.

27. September 13, 1623. In Hoffmann, *Briefe Grosser Deutscher*, p. 20.

28. February 17, 1625. In ibid., p. 21.

29. November 4, 1823. In ibid., p. 42.

30. February 24, 1825. In ibid., pp. 42–43.

31. Cited by Cornelia N. Moore, *The Maiden's Mirror: Reading Material for German Girls in the Sixteenth and Seventeenth Centuries* (Wiesbaden, 1987), pp. 105–106.

32. "Dr. Gregory: A Father's Legacy to His Daughters," in *The Young Lady's Pocket Library, or Parental Monitor* (1790), cited in Pollock, *A Lasting Relationship*, p. 256.

33. If not the mother's maiden name, then apparently that of a male relative known to young Körner, who, like his father, remained chaste until marriage.

34. "In disem einzigen Punkte verwildert sind."

35. June 12, 1808. In Hoffmann, *Briefe grosser Deutscher*, p. 175.

36. *Letters of Lord Chesterfield to His Son* (London, 1929), April 19, 1749, p. 105.

37. Two practical Englishmen of genius. Charles Robert Cockerell (1788–1863), famed architect (with Covent Garden and a wing of Cambridge University Library among his credits), traveled widely in Greece and Asia Minor (he was a member of the team that discovered the Aegina marbles, the first of his many important finds) and belonged to numerous European archeological academies, including that of Bavaria. Leslie Stephen and Sidney Lee, eds., *Dictionary of National Biography*, vol. 4 (Oxford, 1968), pp. 651–654. Richard Cobden (1804–1865) was a merchant and popular statesman, enormously successful in the calico business. Self-taught in many disciplines, he advocated free trade and wrote popular pamphlets on European relations. Ibid., pp. 604–610.

38. From Blankenese (November 19, 1910). In Hoffmann, *Briefe Grosser Deutscher*, pp. 321–322.

6. FAMILY ARCHIVES

1. Funeral sermons memorialized deceased family members and served as a public record of their lives. They were particularly popular among Lutheran laity in the late sixteenth and seventeenth centuries. Reading through a century's worth of such sermons, and carefully observing the household members present at the increasingly private death scene, scholars of these sources believe they can pinpoint the very decades in the seventeenth century when the nuclear family became a self-conscious entity, distinct from other members of the household. See Rudolf Lenz, ed., *Leichenpredigten als Quelle historischer Wissenschaften*, vol. 1 (Cologne, 1975), esp. pp. 36–51. For medieval "forerunners" of this genre, ibid., p. 293, n. 4; Lenz, "Emotion and Affektion," pp. 121–146.

2. "Gefühlsbetont." *Die Familie in der deutschen Stadt des späten Mittelalters* (Heidelberg, 1980), p. 45. On the scope of German biographical and autobiographical sources between 1400 and 1700, see, in addition to Beer *(Eltern und Kinder)*, T. Klaiber, *Die deutsche Selbstbiographie* (Stuttgart, 1921); Georg Steinhausen, *Geschichte der Deutschen Kultur* (Leipzig, 1929); Georg Misch, *Geschichte der Autobiographie*, vol. 4, part 2 (Frankfurt am Main, 1969); Ernst W. Zeeden, *Deutsche Kultur in der frühen Neuzeit* (Frankfurt am Main, 1968), pp. 479–481; and Kaspar von Greyerz, "Religion in the Life of German and Swiss Autobiographers (Sixteenth and Early Seventeenth Centuries)," in Greyerz, ed., *Religion and Society in Early Modern Europe, 1500–1800* (London, 1984), pp. 223–241. Excerpts from both well-known and obscure sources can be found in Georg Steinhausen, ed., *Deutsche Briefe des Mittelalters*, vol. 1, *Fürsten und Magnaten, Edle und Ritter* (Berlin, 1899), and vol. 2, *Geistliche und Bürger* (Berlin, 1907); Christian

Meyer, ed., *Ausgewählte Selbstbiographien aus dem 15. bis 18. Jahrhundert* (Leipzig, 1897); Werner Mahrholz, *Deutsche Selbstbekenntnisse: Zur Geschichte der Selbstbiographie von der Mystik bis zum Pietismus* (Berlin, 1919); Marianne Beyer-Frölich, *Deutsche Selbstzeugnisse,* vol. 4, *Aus dem Zeitalter des Humanismus und der Reformation* (Leipzig, 1931), and vol. 5, *Aus dem Zeitalter der Reformation und der Gegenreformation* (Leipzig, 1932; rpt. 1964); Horst Wenzel, *Die Autobiographie des Späten Mittelalters und der frühen Neuzeit,* vol. 1, *Die Selbstdeutung des Adels,* and vol. 2, *Die Selbstdeutung des Stadtbürgertums* (Munich, 1980); Hans J. Gernentz, *Ritter, Bürger und Scholaren: Aus Stadtchroniken und Autobiographien des 13. bis 16. Jahrhunderts* (Berlin, 1980), esp. pp. 245–254; Theodor Brüggemann, *Handbuch zur Kinder- und Jugendliteratur: Vom Beginn des Buchdrucks bis 1570* (Stuttgart, 1986); Ulrich Herrmann et al., *Bibliographie zur Geschichte der Kindheit, Jugend und Familie* (Munich, 1980). For English family sources, see Houlbrooke, *English Family Life.*

3. The phrase is Mathias Beer's. *Eltern und Kinder,* p. 39.

4. Ibid., pp. 41–44, 52–55, 63.

5. "Die unmittelbare Aeusserungen wirklichen Menschen." *Der Wandel deutschen Gefühlslebens seit dem Mittelalter* (Hamburg, 1895), p. 4. Steinhausen edited important volumes of such collections to demonstrate his point, among them *Briefwechsel Balthasar Paumgartners des Jüngeren und seiner Gattin Magdalena, geb. Behaim (1582–1598)* (Tübingen, 1895) and *Deutsche Privatbriefe des Mittelalters,* vols. 1 and 2 (Berlin, 1899). See Beer's discussion of letters as a source: *Eltern und Kinder,* pp. 86–89, 98–105, 111–112, 134–141, 168–184; "Ehealltag im späten Mittelalter. Eine Fallstudie zur Rekonstruktion historischer Erfahrungen und Lebensweisen anhand privater Briefe," *Zeitschrift für Württembergische Landesgeschichte* 53 (1994): 101–123;

and "'Wenn ich eynen naren hett zu eynem man, da fragen dye freund nit vil danach': Private Briefe als Quelle für die Eheschliessung bei den stadtbürgerlichen Familien des 15. und 16. Jahrhunderts," in Hans-Jürgen Bachorski, ed., *Ordnung und Lust: Bilder von Liebe, Ehe und Sexualität in Spätmittelalter und Früher Neuzeit* (Trier, 1990), pp. 72–94.

6. The historian who consults the multivolume Paston family letters on fifteenth-century England, or the multivolume Weinsberg papers on sixteenth-century Cologne and northern Germany, or the multivolume Zimmer chronicle on the sixteenth-century southern German nobility finds not only a window onto the immediate subjects, but an elaborate introduction to their larger communities as well. *The Paston Letters, 1422–1509,* 6 vols., ed. James Gairdner (New York, 1900; 1965); *The Paston Letters,* 2 vols., ed. Norman Davis (Oxford, 1999); *Das Buch Weinsberg: Kölner Denkwürdigkeiten aus dem 16. Jahrhundert,* 5 vols., ed. Konstantin Höhlbaum et al. (Leipzig, Bonn, 1886–1926); Joseph Stein, *Hermann von Weinsberg als Mensch und Historiker* (Cologne, 1917); *Die Chronik der Grafen von Zimmern,* 3 vols., ed. Hans Martin Decker-Hauff (Sigmaringen, 1964–1972); Beat Jenny, *Graf Froben Christoph von Zimmern: Geschichtsschreiber-Erzähler-Landesherr* (Lindau, 1959).

ACKNOWLEDGMENTS

I wish to thank the following for kind assistance and encouragement in the development of *Ancestors:* Donna Bouvier, Aida Donald, Scott Hendrix, H. C. Erik Midelfort, Andrea Ozment, Laura Smoller, and Elizabeth Suttell.

INDEX

marriage, 46; and sex, 121n23. *See also* Sentiment

Equality: and marriage, 3, 20, 22, 36–38, 132n46; and women, 14, 15; and children, 22

Erikson, Erik, 57, 64

Family: modern vs. premodern, 2–4; evolution of, 2–4, 9–12, 13–14, 16–21, 44–45; nuclear, 3, 14, 151n1; and society, 5–6, 11–12, 153n6; as moral experiment, 6; and individual, 7, 8, 18; and state, 8, 15, 110; and sentiment, 11; and morality, 13; open lineage, 18–19; restricted patriarchal nuclear, 19; closed domesticated nuclear, 20; ancient, 45–47; medieval, 47–49; and religion, 110; and Protestantism, 122n34; and Luther, 128n28

Fathers, 59, 62, 73, 74, 115n2, 145n52. *See also* Husbands; Men; Parents

Fischart, Johann, 37–38

Flandrin, Jean-Louis, 15–18, 49, 52

Foundling home, 62–63

Fulgentius of Ruspe, 57

Games. *See* Play

Gauss, Carl Friedrich, 91–93

Gauss, Eugen, 91, 93

Generalization. *See* Representativeness

Girls, 75–76, 93–99, 146n60. *See also* Children

Government. *See* State

Hamann, Johann Georg, 88–90

Hildegard of Bingen, 134n7

History, study of, 1–2, 5–9, 63–65, 104–112. *See also specific historians*

Home: and work, 3, 11, 14, 115n2; child's leaving of, 9–10, 75–76, 146n60; and women, 24, 25, 26, 29–30, 31–32, 39, 42, 48–49; and Lutheranism, 31–32; and marriage, 38; for foundlings, 62–63; and state, 129n29

Husbands: and oppression, 15, 16, 26, 41; and companionship, 16, 20; and Protestantism, 31, 128n27; and Luther, 37; as sun, 37, 38; and state, 41, 129n29; and Roman marriage, 46; and medieval marriage, 48, 49. *See also* Marriage; Men

Imitation, 69

Individual, 7, 8, 14, 17, 18, 69

Infanticide, 53, 61–65, 140nn18,19, 141n23

Inheritance, 12, 37, 47

Isidore of Seville, 57

Johann II, Count Palatine, 93–95

Joseph, Saint, 59, 62

Kessler, Johannes, 61

Körner, Karl Theodor, 99

Krause, Johann, 82, 83

Krause, Karl, 82–83

Law: and women, 25–28, 46, 126n17;
and marriage, 41, 46; Roman, 46, 58;
and children, 58, 74; and infanticide,
140n19, 141n23
Letters, 104–105. *See also* Archives
Locke, John, 20
Love, 17, 46, 109. *See also* Emotion;
Sentiment
Luther, Martin: and marriage, 31, 32,
35, 36; and prostitution, 36; and
Katherina von Bora, 37; and family,
128n28
Lutheranism, 31–32

MacFarlane, Alan, 133n1
Manual, confessional, 16, 17
Marriage: and equality, 3, 20, 22, 36–38,
37–38, 132n46; and women, 15, 16,
24–26, 36–38, 39–41, 46–47; and
companionship, 16, 133n1; and Catholic Church, 16, 17–18, 34, 51–52;
and Puritanism, 19–20; and Protestantism, 19–20, 35–38, 55; reasons
for, 19–20, 122n35; and work, 24;
and Luther, 31, 32, 35, 36; and
Lutheranism, 31–32; popularity
of, 33–35; clandestine, 34; clerical,
35; court for, 36; and divorce, 37;
and home, 38; authority in, 41; and
law, 41; and sex, 41; and Roman
law, 46; and religious women, 50;
age of, 75; companionate, 133n1
Mary, 59, 62
Maschke, Erich, 104
Maurice, Saint, 77–78

Men: and oppression, 15, 128n27; and
companionship, 16; representation
by, 27–28; and Luther, 37; guardianship of, 46; and property, 47; and education, 93. *See also* Fathers; Husbands
Mitterauer, Michael, 13–14
Morality: and family, 13; and women,
16; and population rate, 47; and children, 74–75; advice on, 83–85, 93,
99–100
Mortality, child, 11, 19, 59–60, 61,
119n12, 139n14. *See also* Infanticide
Mothers: and contraception, 50–51; image of, 59, 62; and class, 66–67, 68;
and child rearing, 73, 74, 145n52. *See
also* Parents

Newcome, Henry, 80
Nobility, 49
Nuns, 39, 50

Parents: attitude toward children, 9–10,
11, 14, 54–55, 56, 59–70, 139n15; and
rights vs. duties, 16; and child as individual, 17; and contraception, 50–
51; image of, 59, 62; and sentiment,
59–60; and class, 66–67, 68; and
child rearing, 70, 73–75, 76, 145n52,
146n56; and child's work, 73, 76; and
advice, 77–103; and child's failures,
80–81
Peasantry, 48–49

Swaddling, 19, 20, 65–66
Syphilis, 36

Tucher, Katherina, 78
Tucher, Linhart, 77, 78, 79

Wet-nursing, 19, 20, 66–68, 143n39
Wives: and oppression, 15, 16, 26, 41;
and companionship, 16, 20; and
equality, 24–26; as moon, 37, 38; and
state, 41; and Roman marriage, 46;
and medieval marriage, 47, 48–49.
See also Women
Women: and equality, 14, 15; oppression
of, 15, 16, 23, 26–27, 29–30, 31–32,
38–39, 40–42, 42, 49; and marriage,
15, 16, 24–26, 36–38, 39–41, 46–47;
and morality, 16; and punishment, 16,
26; and economy, 23–24, 28–29, 47,
127n19; and work, 23–25, 27–30, 32,
38–40, 42, 43, 46–47, 126n17, 127n19;
and home, 24, 25, 26, 29–30, 31–32,
39, 42, 48–49; and business, 24–25,
27–28; medieval, 24–28, 32–33, 38–
39; and law, 25–28, 126n17; and citizenship, 26; and property, 26, 27, 28,

46, 47; and sex, 26, 134n7; and state,
26, 40–42; and crime, 26–27, 63; and
male representation, 27–28; and
Protestantism, 30, 31–33, 55; and religion, 30, 31–33, 39, 55; and
Lutheranism, 31–32; and prostitution, 33, 34; religious, 39, 50; self-
perception of, 39, 40; and education,
39–40, 93; and wealth, 40, 46; Roman, 46–47; and class, 48–49, 66–67,
68; and patriarchy, 48–49; and infanticide, 62, 63, 140n18
Woodforde, John, 81, 82
Woodforde, Mary, 81–82
Woodforde, Samuel, 81, 82
Work: and home, 3, 11, 14, 115n2; and
economy, 23–24, 28–29, 34, 47,
127n19; and women, 23–25, 27–30,
32, 38–40, 42, 43, 46–47, 126n17,
127n19; and marriage, 24; and
children, 69–70, 73, 75, 76, 144n44;
choice of, 70, 144n44; advice on, 84,
87, 91–93. *See also* Apprenticeship;
Service
Wunder, Heide, 29, 30, 38, 129n29,
132n46

·